Mayhem Mirth and Mastery

Memoirs Of Single Parenting

Caleen Diedrick

Table of Contents

Acknowledgement

irstly I must thank God for his continued guidance and grace as I traverse this life.

I've been blessed in so many ways by some many different persons who were instrumental in the creation of this my first book.

Special thanks to:
Trishan Haughton who helped me to start my blog 5 years ago which was my first step to bring this book to life; Harriet Clarke who use to proof read my blogs; Stacey Palmer my editor; Denecia Green, a fabulous young author who helped me navigate the nuisance of self-publishing; Noran Price the awesome graphic designer responsible for my book cover and Phyllis Williams, artist for the cover picture.

Special mention must be made of my beautiful daughter Janique who changed my life in such a profound way. I love you beans.

Lastly, I must thank my ex Husband Rene for providing me with this experience to pen my first best seller.

Part I

Mayhem

Chapter 1

The Beginning

Me on my wedding day

I got married on July 14, 2001; the day was beautiful. The marriage, however, was a tumultuous one filled with many, many, challenges. Thank God, however, that time is the master of all healing, because today, I look back and laugh as this marriage was clearly the manifestation of where we both were mentally. It wasn't all for naught, because the union became the catalyst that would set in motion many life changing events that took me to murky depths and awe-inspiring heights.

Chapter 2

Pandemonium

He was immature and manic depressive;
I was immature and idealistic
… enter PANDEMONIUM.

During the first year of the marriage our arguments were epic, to say the least. We had regular quarrels; so much so we often left the apartment and go for a drive in order for our cursing and screaming to be out of earshot of our neighbors. One night in particular we drove up to Cherry Gardens and parked close to someone's house in deep discussion over our last conflict when the police pulled up behind us. They asked us to step out of the car with both hands in the air; I was taken aside and asked if I was o.k. and if I was there against my will or if he was being violent. I answered no to all of the questions and told them that he was my husband and that we were having an argument and decided to drive out and talk about it. We came to the area because we thought it would be safer than parking at some lonely location. We all had a good laugh and they told us we had to leave, because a resident of the street we had parked on called them when he noticed that the car was just parked for over twenty minutes with occupants.

We may have laughed that night, but I soon came to realize the magnitude of the demon that was depression. I saw a 6 feet able-bodied, 195 pounds chiseled to the hilt Adonis struggle to find the will to get out of bed in the mornings. This was one of the things we argued about. I would get up at 5.30 in the mornings to begin my day. My routine involved waking him, making breakfast, packing lunch and showering – all in that order. Even after completing the routine, which lasted around an hour, he would still be in bed – refusing to budge.

No matter how much we spoke and quarreled about it, nothing changed. We always managed to get into the car at 7:45 every single morning, even though he needed to get to work at 8 a.m. To prevent him being very late, we drove like bats out of hell mounting sidewalks and driving through malls (I swear we were one of the reasons the malls on Constant Spring Road now chain off their entrances and exits in the early morning). Despite all this, he still could not manage to get out of bed.

The depression was cyclical, and I used to watch helplessly as he lost interest in all of the things he loved (the gym, fishing and the occasional party). This became even more evident around March when his birthday rolled around, as he was just a shell of himself. I watched in absolute shock and dismay as his beautiful body disappeared after three weeks of him barely eating because he had lost his appetite. His mood was erratic, and I struggled to make sense of it all.

In my quest to understand what was happening, I turned to the book, ***"The Power of the Praying Wife" by Stormy Obrian,*** which was given to me by a friend on the night of my bridal shower. I recall vividly reading the book and thinking, "well, if I am praying for all these various parts of his life when in tarnations am I going to find the time to pray for me?" That mindset was short-lived, however, because in short order I became the praying wife. I turned to God in the midst of the all-consuming confusion and despair and prayed and fasted and prayed some more. Nothing helped, it seemed. He started losing his jobs; one after the other they went, because he was perpetually late. When the depression was in full swing (which was most of the year), he could not keep pace with his work. The onset of the manic stage came in December, which is when he'd showed some semblance of normalcy. It was rough, to say the least.

It felt as if we were running out of options. We went from psychiatrist to psychiatrist with each one prescribing a different cocktail of what I deem to be poison to numb the effects of the wicked demon which had cast a very dark and ominous cloud over our dwelling. Evidently, I needed to get a handle on the situation, since nothing worked, so I became obsessed with getting a better understanding of the condition. I read and researched extensively and became very knowledgeable on the matter as well as the drugs available. Nothing worked! Well, nothing did until ….MOTIVAL. I remember this miracle drug because the man CHANGED… it brought about a 180 degree turn in him. He woke up in the mornings on time, and the arguments were significantly less.

He was attentive and alive and more than anything else, he was productive at work and school. It was amazing! For a while during the second year of the marriage, we felt normal.

The actual pregnancy test ...yes I saved it

Not very long after that, things changed. I became pregnant in the third year and wasn't certain how to feel. This wasn't on my agenda at least not for another 3 years. To be honest, I was surprised and somewhat afraid. I was concerned about how this new development would affect my plans. While my other girlfriends were busy attending to their bundle of joy, I was focused on school and career. I knew I wanted children, but I also knew I was nowhere near being mentally ready to take the plunge. I was simply going through the motions and doing my regular thing, and then it happened one day – the reality hit. I was faced with the wretched morning sickness in the first month of the pregnancy; nausea had me incapacitated hanging face down over the toilet. It was then the ENORMITY of my situation struck me like a ton of bricks. I was carrying a life. I was going to be a MOTHER. SHITTTT!!!!!

19

Chapter 3

Alone

"It's knowing no joy
Feeling no pleasure
Seeing no light
It's lifeless
It's passive
Morbid
It's me"[1]

I was sitting in the traffic when the torrents of tears came. Four months had passed since the separation from my husband: our daughter was now 5 months old. But how did I get here?

Rewind...

I had a great pregnancy. My baby was developing nicely, and I was lifting weights and working out every day. At 6 ½ months

---

[1] *Excerpt from the Peom "Alone" by Chfev*

I went away to shop for all things baby and my expanding waistline. I came back two weeks later and went into labor.

On November 5th, I had a caesarean section. When I woke up from that, I was in excruciating pain, but all that vanished when my husband brought our daughter to see me. She was beautiful… I did the instant look-over checking for everything including the full complement of fingers and toes. I then kissed the life I had nurtured with tears in my eyes. Since my baby came early, she was quickly returned to the incubator; she was 3 lbs 8 oz. She would spend the next 3 weeks in the hospital as the doctors wouldn't release her until her weight got to 5 lbs. In spite of being premature, she was very healthy; she shocked the doctors week after week with her rapid weight gain.

Janique, my precious baby girl, was released from the hospital in late November weighing 5 lbs 5 oz.

I was bonding with our child and had adjusted to having her around. I fell into the role of mother naturally and developed a seamless pattern with her. My husband, on the other hand, seemed more and more estranged from her. In the initial stages, I thought he was afraid of holding her because she was so tiny. After a while, it became apparent that he simply had no connection to her. After a month of noticing of observing the situation, I pointed it out to him and gently asked what was happening. He could not give me a reason, so I left it alone. During the pregnancy, I had started to embrace the idea that the marriage wasn't going to survive. His constant companion, depression, was back in full force as the company that manufactured the miracle drug that so helped him suddenly went out of business. Nothing else worked, and soon the arguments started to rear their ugly heads. At this point, I was no longer an active participant as I was exhausted and sick to death of the roller coaster that defined our union and so emotionally I made my exit from our relationship.

It was while having brunch at my girlfriend's baby christening that I received a call from him to inform me that he was moving out and wanted to work on the relationship away from the matrimonial home. I told him to handle his business and hung up the phone without a second thought of our conversation. I exhaled, kissed Janique on the forehead and enjoyed the rest of the day. I was relieved.

A month later we came to an impasse while we were in counseling explaining the issues that plagued our marriage; with the help of family, we decided to try again. Needless to say, it was a COLOSSAL mistake. Within three weeks, the proverbial crap hit the fan and the dolly house came crumbling down. He lost the job he had the longest; and when he explained what had happened, I was livid. I felt he could have handled the situation better and kept thinking about Janique and how we were going to manage. We had our biggest argument yet and he asked me to leave. I left with my daughter the same night and never looked back.

Later he came around trying to reconcile but I was finished. I had vowed when I left the apartment that under no circumstances would I ever return to this man. He made valiant attempts to get me to reconcile, I told him that he was free to see Janique as long as I had a few hours' notice but our chapter had ended.

I had found an apartment and was as happy as a lark to be free of the weight of our marriage. When it was clear to my husband that I was resolute in my decision, he stopped visiting Janique. I arranged for him to deposit money for her in an account, and he disappeared.

Months went by, and I felt nothing. I was numb. I had not shed a tear in the face of everything that had happened, and I was concerned. I knew I needed to grieve but the tears just wouldn't come. Then it happened. One unsuspecting night, I flew out of my sleep drenched in sweat; my heart was pounding out of my chest and all my attention was on Janique sleeping peacefully in her crib. I started to hyperventilate and had to cover my mouth to suffocate the scream that was in my throat.

 "Jesus Christ; have mercy!" I thought. I have this child to take care of by myself? How could this be happening? I did it the "right way?" I got married BEFORE I had the baby and now in a twisted turn of fate I was a single mother… what the FUCK?

There they were – the mystery tears. Suddenly, they came consistently for four weeks. I wept like my family had been annihilated. Because of this, I never left my sunglasses, as the tears came unsuspectingly and at different points of the day. I could be in business meetings and start to tear up. I cried in the supermarket. I cried at work, and now I sat crying in the traffic, crippled with fear and confusion, clinging desperately to my logics and ideals and struggling to accept that this horror movie was in fact MY new reality.

Chapter 4

Clouds of Light

They look so small and frail
But they are so great and magnificent.
They are born of the same womb
That birthed the cosmos
And knitted together the galaxies.

If you could see them as they truly are,
You would be astounded
You would see not little children
But dancing clouds of light
Energy in motion
Swimming in an ocean of love.

They are so much more
Than what you see
As are you.[2]

---

[2] From *The Parent's Toe Te Ching 1999*

It is said that God never gives us more than we can bear. With that being said, most of us only come to this conclusion when we find ourselves in the crucible and manage to come out better than we went in. After accepting my new role of single mother, some of the fear and confusion slowly started leaving me. In this painful new situation, I stumbled upon a profound healing. Without warning, I was being taken over by the magnificence of my wonderful daughter. Janique was an amazing baby. She was always agreeable and quiet. Her stillness and pleasant disposition uplifted my spirit in the darkest moments.

At each stage of her growth, since birth, she was an easy baby. Despite being born a preemie, the first six months of her life was a breeze. She went from spending one month in the hospital right after being born to flourishing and meeting all her developmental milestones with flying colors. She was exactly where she should be, and by the six month mark, Janique was a babbling, curious and pleasant baby, despite being weaned off the breast at four months two weeks. According to my parents, Janique was "begging her feet to walk"

I had no idea what emotions Janique would evoke each day, but her antics injected rejuvenating energy. I was enthralled by her progress as I was told that her development would be slower because she was premature. Instead, her effortless way of being taught me many lessons. I realized that Janique trusted that I would be responsive to her needs and that her only job was to let me know (usually the few times she cried) that she needed something. I saw the relief and joy that engulfed her when I came to get her when she fussed. I saw the love and appreciation in her eyes when we played, which often manifested itself in the form of a very wet sloppy kiss on my nose, eyes or lips).

I accepted the fact that I did not understand why this was happening to me and came to the realization through Janique's responses that somehow all would be well. My "dancing cloud of light" was showing me that I needed to trust even when nothing made sense.

Chapter 5

The End of the Road

I sat across a table listening to my lawyer present my requests as it pertains to child support. It had been two and half years since I had last seen my husband, and here we were now getting divorce. So many things had happened in the time we were apart. Janique was thriving and I was constantly being schooled by the things she did and eventually said. This initiated a new level of growth and development for me.

Janique's antics kept me amused and pensive all at once. I remember one Sunday morning I was running late for church, and she wanted to play. She came to me in the bathroom and said, "Mommy let's play hide and seek and when you find me you must grab me and say I got you". My response was, "Child we are going to be late for church so let's do this hide and seek bit later". Before I completed my sentence she had manage to maneuver herself under the bed and was shouting out a reminder of her directives. I realized at this point that I might as well indulge her, so I pretended to search for her everywhere in the house leaving under the bed for last. When I got under the bed I did as she had instructed, and we both had a good laugh. Once she had gotten her game of hide and seek out of her system, she became more amenable.

This moment of indulgence impacted me deeply in the sense that Janique not only asked for what she wanted but anticipated a favorable response in spite of what I was saying.. This act reinforced for me the importance of asking for what you want but more importantly, mentally and physically getting oneself in "receive mode". , she reiterated, that being in this mode is a superb way of ensuring that your requests are answered. In this simple moment, another life lesson also became apparent - the importance of indulging your loved ones. I noted how pliable and receptive she became towards me when I gave her something that mattered to her. I was yet again reminded of how powerful an agent this small and simple act was of giving someone what they asked for, when and how they ask for it to be delivered (no matter how insignificant one might consider it to be).

In as much as the lessons came, the challenges also found space in the mix. With each passing day, I developed a deeper appreciation of the old adage "it takes a village to raise a child." In fact, this became my way of life since being a single parent meant that I was I always in need of a few more willing and available villagers. For the first year of her life, Janique was always with me. But I knew that had to change one day, so I finally built up the courage to send her to preschool when she was 9 months; it didn't matter though, because I still felt overwhelmed. There were days that I just wanted some time to myself to do me (nails, shop, party or sit at home and relax).

Even though I enjoyed being a mom to Janique, there were days when I became angry at the thought of parenting on my own when she had a father who lived on the same island and within close enough proximity.   My frustration reached boiling point one night when I came home from work very tired. I had had a really trying day and went to get Janique from school. We had sat in traffic for what seemed like an eternity. Added to that, I had to struggle up the stairs to my apartment bearing several bags on one arm and Janique resting on the other.

By the time we entered the apartment, she was half asleep, so I laid her down on my bed. I then went into the kitchen to make dinner and was startled when I heard Janique hit the ground and started to wail at the top of her lungs. Within seconds I was in the room, and grabbed her off the floor. She was screaming as I checked for cuts and bruises, while simultaneously trying to console her. Everything fell apart for me then, and the flood gates opened. My attempt to console a crying Janique was met by my own all-encompassing sadness. I wept bitterly out of frustration and fatigue. Now that I look back, I recognize that in that moment we were both crying because we were frightened and hurting.

The sadness and anger came intermittently. Along with that mix of emotions, I also had a recurring thought about being in the supermarket and seeing my husband. I envisioned him coming over to say something to me or touching Janique, which would awaken my sleeping savage beast! I also envisioned me launching a vicious, violent attack thereby obliterating this creature! God! I wanted to break skin and bones so badly that I anticipated this chance-meeting and even prayed for it. This, however, did not come to fruition, because God, in his infinite wisdom, did not facilitate this wish, and I was never lucky enough to run into to him. Interestingly, everyone else in my circle would run into him and tell me. That became too often and too much for me to handle, so I had to start telling friends and acquaintances to refrain from reporting the all too regular sightings of my ex-husband.

Now, here we were sitting at the table with both our lawyers chatting feverishly back and forth. The moment was surreal, and I could not articulate what I was feeling. At no point could he make eye contact with me, so he chanced furtive glances in my direction. I looked at him and wondered, "What manner of man is this?" I sat there trying hard to understand what made this man decide he did not wish to have any contact with his child? I wondered how he justified not seeing her to himself year after year knowing that I was always open to that. Then the real question came. It rose from my toes, cold and heavy lodging itself firmly in my chest, "What manner of woman was I to have attracted this to my life?"

Chapter 6

Happy Mother's Month

I am usually very reflective around Mother's Day. So this particular mother's day was no different. Janique had recently turned 9 years old, and I felt a sense of pride and accomplishment for having made it this far. I stumbled into the role of motherhood; Lord knows that the journey has been a colorful one fraught with trials, tribulations and unexpected triumphs.

During this journey, I have had to face myself. I have had to confront issues about myself that I wouldn't have had reasons to look at before, at least not in a way that would have stimulated the level of introspection this circumstance provoked. This new role of mothering shook me to my core. The situations I had to deal with each day stirred fears, misconceptions and memories lying dormant under my composed veneer.

My Challenges

As Janique got older, I was forced to deal with my impatience. I came face to face with it when she started school and her homework needed to get done. I would be in the middle of explaining some new principle and completely lose it, because I believed she should have been able to understand the concepts we were reviewing. As a result, I became upset with what I deemed to be her lack of understanding. One day, in the midst of my usual tirade, she spoke to me. With balls of tears streaming down her face she said, "Mommy, stop shouting; I won't get it if you keep shouting." She held my gaze and then said softly with tears coursing down her face, "I don't like it when you shout at me; it hurts my feelings". I felt like I had been kicked in the solar plexus. On previous occasions when she had asked me to stop shouting I would tell her she needed to focus and that I would not be shouting if she would only pay attention. When she spoke to me that day the absurdity of what I used to tell her sank in. Lesson learnt!

As the facilitator of personal development workshops, I am privy to how people tend to blame their negative reactions on another person or the situation they are in at the given moment; this type of blame game is typically the general consensus. Most persons are usually very convinced that had it not been for their current situation, they would not angrily lash out and hurt the other person. Because of my familiarity with this type of situation, I was usually successful with helping people, through the use of various techniques, to take ownership of their role in the demise of the situation. Even though I understood these situations and had success in rectifying them, here I was doing the very same thing to my daughter. On this day, however, I heard her plea and in the process saw my own shortcomings; I apologized and told her that I would be more mindful moving forward. While I can't say that I have completely perfected my response in scenarios of this kind, I have since calmed down considerably with the shouting. Change has happened.

Paranoia

I was molested as a child. The first time I openly spoke about it was in the final year of high school (6th form). A group of us decided to have a party at a friends' house; in the midst of the festivities, one of the girls said she needed to talk. She wanted our advice on something that had happened to her. She then told us how her boyfriend whom she had recently separated from came by her house in an attempt to reconcile. She said he made sexual advances towards her and she told him she was not interested but that he had held her down and forcibly had sex with her. She wanted to know if this was rape. We all sat dumbfounded looking at her as she asked for our input. Everyone agreed that it was rape. This conversation opened Pandora's Box. All the girls in the room had been raped. One by one they told their story (some for the very first time) of how cousins, uncles, step fathers and strangers had viciously taken their innocence. One of the girls whose story impacted me related her ordeal in the third person. With absolutely no emotions present, she told us how she had been violated by two men on a school trip overseas.

As far as I could tell, my own situation did not affect me too much - psychologically or otherwise; but as it pertains, to Janique I became HYPER-VIGILANT. Everyone was viewed as a potential predator, and I had extraordinary struggles leaving her with a baby sitter. In public, however, I allowed her to roam about freely and mingle, but I watched her like a hawk. I had a hand full of friends that I felt comfortable with, but every other scenario – no matter the person - made me nervous. The paranoia ate at me like a terminal illness. After two years, I took some time to really examine what was going on with me and came to the realization that I was so very afraid of the worst happening to my child; the stories I heard, plus my own, scarred me and in turn affected how I parented my own child. Without any real threat being obvious, I walked around in fear for her. I knew this was an unhealthy way to exist, so I decided that it was time to trust that which I considered to be higher than myself. I decided it was time to trust God. I went into deep prayer and asked for guidance, and eventually it came. As a result, I surrendered and let go of so much of the fears I had given free residence in my head and felt lighter and happier.

For me, parenting served as the catalyst for many changes that happened and were about to happen in my life. Parenting has caused me to take a longer and harder look at some of my negative persistent preoccupations and have brought about new perspectives and ultimately some peace of mind. While I can't and won't tell you that I am completely cured of my concerns around Janique's safety or that I have mastered the art of navigating this role from a healthier, functional place all the time, I can say with conviction that today, I am in a much better space.

As I have grown in my own parenting quest, I now have a newfound appreciation for mothers. I so understand the sacrifices they make in a bid to create a safe and nurturing environment for their children. I understand the worry and the days and nights spent in prayer asking for help to triumph over the many trials that present themselves. I understand the selflessness required to ensure their children's well-being. I SALUTE all the wonderful mothers who continue to feed, support and uplift our future generation. HAPPY MOTHER'S MONTH.

Worksheet No. 1

1. So many mothers have been the victims of one type of abuse or another – be it sexual, emotional, verbal or physical. If you were a victim of any form of abuse, has it affected the way you parent your child/children? Really think about this question and ask yourself, "have I become more overly-protective or have I been very harsh to my child/children with my words and behaviour as a result of the abuse sustained? Explain how.

2. Does the abuse affect the way you relate to the men in your relationship? If so, explain how.

3. Have you sought help to process the abuse you experienced? If not, why?

4. As parents, some of us don't believe we need to apologise to our child/children for the painful things we say to them or how we treat them.

Have you ever apologized to your child/children? If so, how did it make you feel?

Chapter 7

Matters Of The Heart

Part 1

"Life is 10% of what happens to you and 90% of how you react to it"

My ex-husband represented some major "firsts" for me. He was my first sexual experience, first "real" relationship, first marriage, the father of my first (and probably only) child so when we separated I wasn't the same person; by this time, too much had transpired between us. Like most newlyweds, I had come into the marriage with a certain level of idealistic innocence - wide eyed and bushy tailed with foolish ideals and expectations. The total opposite occurred in the end; I walked away torn, angry and guarded. Although in the end, I was emotionally ready to leave and had no reservations about doing so, I knew by then that it would take a heartfelt connection with another man to gauge the amount of baggage I was carrying.

My Ten Percent

In my late teens to early twenties I had a lot of male friends. When it became apparent that I wasn't interested in getting physical or being involved in a relationship, I became a part of the crew. I was their confidant and sounding board. They spoke to me about their conquests and challenges with women, and I paid attention. I made a decision there and then that none of these immature, sex-craved, stripes-seeking, Neanderthals was worthy of me. On the flip side, all of my girlfriends were sexually active but only one had a relationship that had some substance. Most had this one-sided awkward exchange that seemed to permeate their interactions with men (the women all wanted an emotional connection but were really just getting the physical).

Because of the space I occupied among the guys, my observations shaped my outlook on men; I came to believe that most lacked integrity and were prepared to jeopardize their relationship with the woman they claimed they loved for a bump and grind with her friend or some other available distraction. I had seen this so many times that I resolved that it was necessary to STAND in love as falling in love meant risking peace of mind and your good health.

I was so invested in this thought that I ran head first into the very same situation with the men I had dated before marriage and then my ex-husband was the icing on the cake. During our first separation we met to discuss how we were going to move forward. I remember asking him if he had been with anyone and the man held my face looked into my eyes and told me no.

We had unprotected sex that night because I believed him. Shortly after our last separation I discovered that he had been unfaithful. I knew the young lady and had a conversation with her to confirm that it was true and to find out the extent of my exposure to any sexually transmitted diseases. She spoke candidly after I reassured her that I meant her no harm, physical or otherwise. I then confronted him. He denied it vehemently then after a few days he admitted that it was so. I went to the doctor and got tested for every S.T.I known to man. My heart hardened at the thought that I might have contracted something incurable from him. Truth be told, I premeditated his murder in the event that any one of the tests came back positive. I was grateful that God's mercies prevailed and I was spared any grief when all the tests came back negative.

A few weeks later he asked to come see me to talk things over and proceeded to tell me how much he wanted our relationship. To ensure that we had a chance, he needed to empty his closet. He then told me of the MANY OTHERS that I did not know about. When he spoke I felt no anger, no hurt, no resentment I just sat and listened keenly and as I observed his body language and watched him relive his exploits, I knew there and then, that his philandering ways had nothing to do with me. His face came alive as he spoke of the circumstances surrounding their meeting and where he eventually bedded them down; he was like a man recounting his hunt and capture of a full grown Grizzly bear. Then he said, "Caleen I never meant to hurt you but the only way I can explain my behaviour is to say I am like an alcoholic but my bars are on legs".

In all honesty, I was not the kind of wife that had my head buried in the sand while my husband feasted on the help and the ladies in the neighborhood, so I was curious when he found the time to get up to his antics. He was unlike most men where there are usually tell-tale signs that something is afoot. He and I spoke openly (or so I thought) about the people we met and found interesting and even talked about the attractions we felt for others. He NEVER hung out with the boys neither was he out partying by himself much. He did not receive those after-hours text or phone calls, neither did he need to leave the room to take the call or keep the call succinct in my presence. Furthermore, his calls never broke down into the strained monosyllables, and his phone wasn't his appendage or preoccupation. I started to wonder how I missed all of this. When I asked him he said his activities took place at lunch time or when I didn't accompany him on fishing trips and or when I went overseas. He said he made a point of telling the women he was married and was not involved with anyone long enough to develop emotional ties. They were all just something to do… period. My 10% was now solidified.

Falling in love

Post marriage, I wanted to do the dating game differently. I wanted to view things from the other side. I considered the possibility that I might have been too militant in my earlier years; I wondered if I had held myself too tightly; maybe I just needed to relax and not take things so seriously. I was now open to the idea of something casual. I had a long-time friend that I was attracted to and decided to explore that. It was good in the sense that we were very comfortable with each other, and he understood and respected what I wanted. We saw each other for a year then I severed the physical ties.

I was in a very good place at that time. I was gainfully employed. I had a new attitude about my life and how things were unfolding and each day I put some more of my past behind me while embracing the gifts of the present. And then out of nowhere it happened.

My first real encounter with love caught me off guard. It happened with a wonderful man that had become my confidant. We met when my ex-husband and I went into his store to purchase a computer. He invited us to his birthday party and from that point he and I became good friends. He was great with Janique and was there for me in the midst of the turmoil with my ex-husband and provided great advice. He worked assiduously with me to let go of the anger I was carrying towards my ex-husband and ensured that I got the necessary intervention to work through my emotional challenges.
All these years he had just been a good friend to me. I had never looked at him in any other light. After a while he expressed that he had feelings for me, but I shunned him every time he mentioned it. Our friendship and connection was like no other, and I cherished it way too much to cross the invisible line into the physical which I felt had the capacity to complicate our seamless fit.

Then one day it happened. He came to my apartment on his way to a presentation dressed in a business suit. He started to relate the day's events to me. It happened almost in slow motion; one minute I was laughing at a joke he was telling, and the next minute I was looking up from what I was doing and saw him – really saw him. I saw his broad shoulders under his well-fitted jacket; I saw his handsome face, his beautifully shaped lips, and the glow of his evenly-toned ebony skin. I looked at him sitting comfortably in my bean bag and SAW a man I had not seen over the years. He looked at me puzzled and asked if I was ok. I told him yes then said, "You're starting to look good to me".

A mischievous smile flashed across his face as he lend forward and said, "About time".

Another year passed before I worked up the courage to explore us, and even then I was still only open to something casual. I was pleasantly surprised when I realized that our bond intensified. He continued to facilitate my healing process by taking me to seminars and workshops that gave me a chance to examine my life from a deeper place. We had managed to maintain our playfulness and easy rapport and I felt great that our friendship had not been compromised. After a few months, he asked me to consider the possibility of seeing him as something more seriously. I shot the suggestion down and told him no way. There was a lot more to his situation that made it complicated, and I felt that I knew too much about his past to really be able to trust him and so I RAN AWAY. He kept on coming and nothing I said was a good enough reason for him to retreat.

It didn't matter that I did everything that I could have done to prevent it happening, it did. It was while I was in full flight and running to the safety of higher ground that I FELL IN LOVE with him…talk about dramatic irony. It happened when we were in a 6 day seminar that he had hauled me off kicking but not quite screaming, because I was afraid to leave my child with a babysitter. Notwithstanding, the seminar was divine intervention as both of us got the opportunity to explore a lot of our past/present demons and fears. It was while he told the story of his painful childhood that I became conscious of the fact that I was in love with him. Something came over me as I watched him recount the abuse he had faced as a child. My heart did something I can't quite relate in words (even today) and I felt the need to protect him, to wrap him up in my bosom where he could find solace. Although I was hit with this realization, in actuality, I doubled my efforts to put more distance between us but he never lost stride in his pursuit. Finally, a full ten months later when his situation changed drastically, I made the decision to give us a chance…

Enter Fear Fest

For the very first time in my life I was in love. I had loved my ex-husband, but I was aware that he had not gained access to a certain place in my heart. I had securely shut away that place over the years in a bid to stand in love. The examples I had seen of my female friends that claimed to be in love looked like weakness to me. I felt they gave so much of themselves away to capture the heart of the object of their affection. They seemed to have lost their voice in an effort to become what they thought their men wanted. I was resolute that that way of life was not for me, so much so that I had managed to stay awake and conscious when it came to matters of the heart until now…

When this love happened upon me, I felt out of sorts as well as a heightened sense of being at the same time. In other instances I felt that I had lost control when I could not maintain the emotional distance I used to summon so effortlessly in the past. This feeling added to the excitement and the sense of trepidation that took me over. At times, I did not recognize myself and felt conflicted. At other points, I was on top of the world giggling and frolicking about. Eventually, I settled into the idea of us, and then the tests came.

We started having arguments and misunderstandings that escalated into ugly shouting matches. As soon as we resolved one argument another was waiting in the wings. I became very aware of his responses and behavior, and over a period of time, depending on the nature of our falling out, suspicion crept in. I started to cross-reference some of his behavior to that of my ex-husband and then hyper-vigilance became a way of life for me.

My satellites sprang into action when his phone rang in my presence. I read his body language and could sum up within the first five seconds of him saying hello if it was business, a blast from his past or a female that might have gotten his attention. I needed answers if something seemed out of place, and I had to get the answers right away. Any delay in his response or any response that did not have a logical fit came under heavy scrutiny. I had never been afflicted with this kind of suspicion before, so after a while, I felt the need to talk about this foreign matter that had taken up residence in my mind and chest. I started to feel like one of the unfortunate persons in the movie, **ALIENS,** which had become the host of this awful unknown creature. The wave of suspicion I experienced could only be likened to the birthing process of the alien that having incubated itself into the chest of the person, was splitting their rib cage from the inside to make its entry into the world. I spoke to my girlfriends about it and then I spoke to him. I told him that I realized that some of our arguments exposed the scarring from my experience with my ex-husband and in spite of noticing it I felt somewhat powerless in my attempt to control it. He did not take this information well in the first instance and for a while our differences deepened.

Our relationship not only stirred my sleeping fears, but it agitated a lot of the monsters from his past. It became apparent, in some of our arguments, that his struggles had nothing to do with our present situation but was, instead, a retention from his turbulent past. Our love turned into a slug fest with both us beating each other with our ten percent from yesterday. I was reminded of a song by Junior Kelly *"If love so nice tell me why it hurt so bad"*. Soon, things became raw between us and the tension was palpable. I took the focus off him and who I thought he was being and became cognizant of the fact that this unpleasantness that so resembled my marriage (the arguments) was happening to ME AGAIN. Not only was my 10% alive and well but my 90% (how I was handling my 10%) served to perpetuate the ugliness.

The relationship came to an end after a year, and I was devastated. My introspection had commenced during the latter stages of our relationship and now that we were at the end of it, the root of our conflicts was so much clearer. Our 10% ravaged us, and we triggered each other's latent fears and hurts. None of us could stay present long enough to work through our differences because our differences were the ghosts of our past. Our love had opened up places within us that we had shut away for self-preservation. For us both, these unresolved issues became an illusion bank with both of us making heavy direct deposits.

No words could encapsulate the depth of the hurt I felt. Not only had I lost what felt like the love of my life, but I had lost my most treasured friendship. Things had become so strained between us after the separation that we could only manage to be civil, if we were required to conduct business together. Everything we once had was gone, and I retreated inwards. I was acutely aware of my role in the demise of this relationship; there was no denying how my new found trust issues affected my behavior. In fact, I now had conclusive proof that scarring from my ex-husband was present and even more frightening, admittedly, I had taken him into my today. I had managed to pour old wine into my new wine skin, and it had burst under the pressure.

Worksheet No. 2

1. Have you identified the event/s in your life that created a negative perception of people, love and family? Write about the situation/s.

2. How have these negative perceptions affected the decisions you've made in your love relationships, friendships or business? Explain.

3. Write about the experience(s) that caused you to become distrustful?

4. How did your inability to trust affect you and your relationships?

5. Can you identify your other emotional scars? If so explain

6. What have you done to resolve them?

Chapter 8

The Great Depression

"Let go, and let God".

The year was 2010, and all hell had broken loose.

Jamaica was in the throes of the recession and the N.G.O. I worked for had been dealt a back-breaking blow as all the contracts we had signed to expand our rehabilitation work in the prisons were rescinded. The recession obstructed our ability to get funding in other areas and so the plans to roll out our behavior-modification program in the schools became impossible. For the first time in my work life, I was faced with unemployment. Additionally, my ex-husband had recently lost his job and could no longer pay child support, so all my sources of income had come to a halt. Needless to say, I was an emotional wreck, mangled and heartbroken from the break up with my friend and lover. I was in the biggest crisis of my life thus far and had no idea which way to turn.

Months prior I had seen a reality series that depicted the life of a surfer. In an interview with the some of the world's most renowned surfers, one spoke about the experience of being swallowed up by the gigantic waves most surfers live to ride. He said the power of the wave and the resulting adrenaline rush the surfer experiences is more than he could describe. He went on to explain that the surfer attacks the wave with everything he has, darting in and out as the outer sides of the wave come crashing down. He pointed out that there are times that the sides and the top of the waves are coming down faster than the surfer can propel himself along and he gets sucked in under this huge wall of water. He said this has a disorienting effect on the surfer as the force of the water and the current tends to pull the surfer further underwater than anticipated. The surfer, having lost his bearings, has no idea which way is up. He pointed out that this is a critical time as things can turn tragic and some of the best surfers and swimmers run out of air trying to surface.

This surfer analogy fit my situation exactly. My life had brought me to yet another crossroad and I felt overwhelmed. I was lying face down at this intersection as a result of being hit by the biggest wave of my life to date; I was under water and did not know which way would float me back to the surface. I felt as though I had been knocked off my surfboard and the safety attachment on my ankle had broken loose. I was even more startled because my concept of being in control of my life seemed to have been shot to shit. Still, the fighter in me wouldn't give up, so I swam fast and frantically at times in a bid to surface. After a while, I started swimming slower to catch my bearings. I had read something that said, "When you are lost and confused start paying attention." In the moments when I was able to still the incessant mental din I asked myself, "what am I doing wrong?" and "why is this happening to me?" Different things came to me at different times, but the ongoing task of putting the pieces of the puzzle of my life together still had me in a quandary. I was clueless!

The following are excerpts from my diary which show where my mind was at the time…

Dated 30/6/10

Last year he had taken me to Portland to visit a friend of his. The host took us to Frenchmen Cove for a relaxing day on the beach. Two of her friends met us there. One was full bodied and reserved and the other was petite with a cute face. The latter was talkative and very animated. I noticed that she was drinking heavily; she had over 8 bottles of Magnum for the day. The conversation eventually worked its way around to what was going on with her. She revealed that her best friend who was also her girlfriend had just broken up with her and she was having a hard time dealing with it. Now I don't drink and for the most part I don't smoke but I understand the allure of these stimulants/depressants and how they facilitate the need to for an altered state of mind. In recent times, in light of my present circumstances there is a huge part of me that yearns to be lost in the numbing clutches of weed. Tonight is no different as I sit here musing about human relations. It never ceases to amaze me how two people come together and share wonderful, awe inspiring, earth moving, moments; they share tenderness and sweet intimacy that in many cases some never experience again and they allow their past and ego to destroy it. They close the chapter with anger, bitterness and resentment and some even pass each other in the streets like strangers in the night. I am reminded of the movie **Why Did I get Married 2**, *the psychologist (played by Janet Jackson) and her husband had been having some recurring issues. On one of their customary marriage retreats she announced that they were getting a divorce. She was smiling with all her friends (who were all looking on in absolute shock including her husband) and explained that her soon to be ex hubby and herself would be very good friends so they need not worry about them as all would be well. When I think about the shit storm that unravels between them as the movie unfolds I am saddened because in that movie I saw myself and so many others of us in or freshly out of a relationship. I saw a woman that had received notable acclaim for her work in marriage counselling and could bring reason to everyone else's affairs except her own. I saw a man that loved his wife with all his might and just wanted her to release the past (the death of their son and the guilt she carried for her role in his demise) and show up in their relationship. I saw the battle of the egos that eventually crushed them.*

I saw he and I in this portrayal as our past had been given a position of pre-eminence in our relationship; it sat high and tall between us. I have dissected us from every angle and at this interval I am broken hearted when I consider everything we know and our inability to apply it to us when it mattered. I now see clearly that one can be very well trained to help others (and do a great job at it) but have immense struggles bringing this knowledge and presence of mind to their own situation.

We had spoken on different occasions about what happened between us and it became apparent that he had many unresolved issues over some of the arguments we had and that he blamed me for the demise of our relationship. Nothing I said could get him to understand the fear that had consumed me. I went on to explain that we both contributed to where our relationship was now but I never felt he took ownership of his role in it as he believed that he was only responding to what I was bringing. As a result of this nothing changed or soften between us.

I have watched him tolerate me when we have to work together and it is clear that I have fallen from grace, I had been his queen in heaven and now I felt like the devil in his side. I wondered where his highly touted love went and I observed my internal struggle to let him go mentally as he ran into the arms of his new conquests and play things. Over the months I had searched ardently for work to firstly sort out my finances and secondly to put some distance between us but even the most promising job did not come to fruition. I came to the conclusion that God must have wanted us to work together to get some major things done...ok, I was good with that. My conflict has been with the "feelings" I still have for him. Try as I may I can't figure out why the fucking feelings persist.

I am wondering what the hell is going on. I feel as if I am having an out of body experience as I can't will myself to stop feeling for this man. I have become indifferent towards him when we have to be together but I wake up with him in my thoughts, I go through the day in like manner and before I close my eyes at night he is the last thought. Sometimes I find him so infuriating and I become pissing, hopping mad at him, other times I miss him, oh Lord I miss him. I miss his eyes and the way he once stared at me with love, appreciation and desire. I miss his hugs and the sound he makes when he gathers me up in his arms (like that of total enjoyment, like taking a bite of your favorite food). I miss his kisses and touch, my entire body misses his. I miss our talks, our long talks. I miss his cheese sandwiches and half frozen Kool Aid served in wine glasses. I miss being an integral part of his life. I miss us.

In a bid to protect my bleeding heart I have been trying to amputate the faulty valves but I'm not sure which one is causing the bleeding and so I have been making every attempt to shut the organ/perception of love or whatever down completely. In spite of my best efforts the frigging feelings are still there and surface whenever I see him.

I feel like an idiot, just one big fucking jackass and I hate it. I feel so absolutely stupid. I know if the opportunity presented itself I would put so much distance between us it would be frightening. I would shut away until I was emotionally unaffected by him. But then I realized the irony of my situation in that I would now become one of those people that had something amazing with another and replaced it with nothingness.

There is a part of me that says let the chips fall where they may because the need for peace of mind is paramount and then there is the other side that says I have a personal responsibility to allow the love I feel for this man to supersede our present state of affairs (my blasted heart or the concept of being hurt) and allow the sweetness and realness that was once us to come to forefront.

Dairy 11/07/10

All is still the same. Still no work… no frigging work and the chasm continues to grow between my ex and I. I have been praying in the midst of my despair. I have been asking God for direction. I have been asking Him "what is the lesson in all this?" and "why has it taken so long to reveal itself?"

My prayer tonight was just as urgent and insistent as the others. I wished for an audience with God. I wished it was like a visit to the doctor where you wait your turn to see the person then divulge your concerns. I wanted to stand before Him and fall into His arms and bawl for as long as it took to let go of the hurts and disappointments. I wanted to bawl until my fears disappeared however more than anything else I wanted to be enveloped in His arms, held and hushed. I wanted Him to talk to me and tell me what to do as I felt so lost.

Our journey together (my ex and I) had a profound impact on both of us; we had grown tremendously in our thinking which positively affected how we processed our life events. I could attribute my chief personal growth spurt to having worked with him and becoming immersed in the things he introduced me to, so I couldn't help but wonder with everything we were to each other, why this was happening to us? I had said to God in the midst of my confusion and even in the moments I felt lucid, that his will be done however I started feeling like Lot's wife (the Bible story of Lot leaving Sodom and Gomorrah). I wondered if I had become Lot's wife as a result of my need to understand what the hell was happening. Had I become Lot's wife because I had asked this question so many times? Had I become Lot's wife because of my frustration with the process? Had I become Lot's wife because of the difficulty I had moving on?

I have come to the conclusion after many days and nights in much anguish that I might never be able to make sense of us therefore I have finally accepted what is. I have my good days when peace of mind is like a warm blanket on a very cold night and then there are the bad days where the mental chatter and heart ache deliver a debilitating blow and I am floored, battered and alone. These days are thankfully less and less. I am certain that our situation was meant to teach us and facilitate the process of us giving birth to ourselves and I also know that the persons closest to us have learnt remarkable lessons from our story. I now say God grant me the strength to change the things I can and the ability to trust that you will never take me into something that you can't take me out of in a way that is advantageous to me.

Worksheet No. 3

1. Write about your first love identifying the areas you felt the person hurt you.

2. Write about your first love identifying how this person and the experience with them made you stronger.

Chapter 9

Forgive Those Who Trespass Against Us

After our divorce, my ex-husband disappeared again. I spent the next year consciously working on the anger I felt towards him and then I had an epiphany. It happened during a ride to the country while listening to Dr. Wayne Dyer (That was the first time I was hearing one of his recordings and I fell in love with his work immediately). His message and delivery was so potent and poignant; the man spoke to my soul. In this particular session, Wayne Dyer was recounting the events of his childhood and his absentee father. He talked about his father leaving his mother and his siblings when she was in hospital giving birth to him (Wayne). He said he spent most of his teenage and early adult life trying to find his father and only found him when he had already been dead for a while. He then visited his grave site to verify that he had been acknowledged as his offspring. Upon confirming that, he flew into a rage. He said he cursed his father for nearly two hours for being an abusive husband and father and for abandoning them when they needed him the most. After a while, he said he found himself thanking him and blessing him. He then gave the following scenario. He said he pictured his father having a conversation with God before this life, justifying his reincarnation. In this conversation with God, his father told God that he wanted to come back to teach someone forgiveness and in order to teach this lesson he needed to be horrific to those closest to him.

Dr. Dyer made the point that he had to re-frame the story he had internalized around his father and acknowledged that his absence and the hardships that came out of that reality provided the impetus for the great work he had done and continues to do. It was his (Dr. Dyer's) need to heal himself that influenced his writings and seminars that have so impacted the world. He went on to say that he had to let go the anger he was carrying towards his father because inadvertently he had made him a better man. He then said, "Forgiveness is the fragrance the violet leaves on the heel that crushed it".

Suddenly, it became clear to me; I had an epiphany and the consciousness struck me instantly. It was time to put the anger down; it was time to release my ex-husband. My whole being was transformed as the weight of anger and the other negative emotions it provoked left me. I called him the next day and asked to see him. He didn't immediately agree to meet with me. Six months had gone by before he finally agreed to the meeting. When I saw him he was a small fraction of his usual muscle bound self. He looked nervous, weary and a little uncertain of himself. I quickly reassured him with some humor by telling him that I had left the shot gun at home and only wanted to talk. In our conversation, I explained to him how angry I was and how hurt I felt about the way he handled the situation with Janique. I also explained the work I had done to get to the place where the anger had finally dissipated. I told him that I forgave him for everything that transpired between us; even his absenteeism.

We spent the next couple of hours talking about the different occurrences in our lives and had some hearty laughs over the trials we were both facing in our unemployment. The conversation was light and liberating, and when I was ready to go I asked him for a hug. We embraced for a long time and in that embrace I fed him with my spirit. I fed him unconditional love, I fed him forgiveness and I fed him joy. We parted ways with him promising to keep in touch.

We spoke for two months intermittently, and one day he stopped by my apartment after leaving a job interview. He threw himself down into my bean bag and his verbal diarrhea came in quick bursts. He revealed how desperate he was feeling, given the length of time he had been unemployed. He highlighted all the places he had tried, all the connections and links he had utilized and still nothing. I listened to him tell my own story and just nodded. I told him to diversify his search and keep the faith as that was what I was doing. I then broached the topic of our child. It was the very first time since we separated that I had asked him for an explanation. He lowered his gaze then looked away. I exhaled and waited for his response as I wanted to understand the thinking that informed his behavior He said he had a vague memory of an incident that transpired in the months shortly after our separation.

We had a tiff, because he had stopped by my apartment unannounced. He said he was annoyed that this was a point of conversation and mentally resolved that he did not need this kind of talk.   He went on to explain that Janique would be a part of his life had we still been together but at that specific juncture, he had felt no real connection to her. He said he was overwhelmed with his life and had many regrets in terms of the choices he made regarding school and other things that were impacting him negatively at this point and then the conversation regressed into the myriad of challenges he was up against.

The more he spoke, the more it became obvious that he could not see past his needs. His needs were paramount and he hadn't considered our child. I looked on and said nothing. I just observed that he was being very honest in the moment and I appreciated that. I chided myself for being upset with this man as it was so clear that I had mistaken our marriage and his ability to impregnate me to mean that he possessed the qualities of a good father. I had been angry with him all this time and now it was apparent that I was expecting something that this man didn't have within to give.

He called me about three weeks later to say he had gotten a job as a personal trainer at a gym and promised that he would contribute financially in spite of his meager salary. One month and half went by, and I heard nothing from him. When I called, he started giving me the run-around and then one day I called the gym and was told that he no longer worked there. He stopped taking my calls and only responded by text. I asked about his work situation and was given more hard luck stories about being strapped for cash and unemployed. Two years went by before I found out that he was in fact employed and gainfully so but was dodging his responsibilities. Unlike him, I didn't have the option of dodging, despite sinking under the weight of the bills. I needed to do something and fast.

A New Perspective

About six months into the unemployment I was called to co facilitate a 3-day personal development workshop for a well-established business. During the second day of the session, one of the participants spoke with much venom about the father of her child. She spoke of her time with him and how much she loved and cared for him and that he went overseas to work and forgot about her and their child. I observed her anger turn into rage as she related just how difficult things had become, then I watched her retreat into shame as she talked about the choices she made and the things she ended up doing for money. She wept bitterly hugging herself, rocking back and forth as she recalled selling herself to keep food on the table.

I empathized with her especially in light of my own circumstances and experienced an immense breakthrough; I finally understood something I used to judge some women for. I used to condemn these women as being "loose" and "low class" until I too was a single mother having to survive without an income for a protracted period of time. I saw and felt what some women had to deal with every day and had a unique understanding of their plight now that I was standing in their shoes. My education and work experience afforded me more options than many other ladies in my situation and fortunately I was spared from having to do certain things. Being privy to the intimate details of one of the women I'd normally condemn caused all my judgments to vanish. We worked diligently to help her put her reframe her situation, and through her, I gained a new perspective on my own situation. I was even more mindful of and grateful for the options available to me - real or unrecognized.

My Chicken Coup

I had always been resourceful; as such, I appreciated the need for a "side hustle" even when I was employed. This need to do something went into overdrive the longer the unemployment persisted.

I remembered hearing a story about a woman in conversation with her son. They were very poor and the mother struggled to carve out a living to support them. One day she stood looking in the backyard and called her 15 year old son over to her. She was staring at a heap of scrap board, zinc and mesh wire. She asked him, "What do you see?" he said, "Garbage". She smiled and he asked her what she saw and she said, "A chicken coup".

I came home one day after taking Janique to school and was miserable beyond words over the lack of work. I had sent resumes everywhere that aligned with my qualifications and had exhausted all of my contacts, my parents' contacts and my friends' contacts. I had turned on the television and was flipping through the channels when I saw an advertisement for edible arrangements and was instantly slapped in the face by inspiration. Two months before I had done a personal development workshop with the Government and was expecting a cheque. I had done a course in floral arrangement some years prior and decided I was going to buy fruits and make some edible arrangements. I could barely contain myself. I took half the money I received from the workshop and purchased fruits, containers, plastic wrap, foam, skewers, decorative accents and cutters. I spent a day learning the rudiments of this kind of arrangement then designed a flyer and posted it on Facebook. Mother's Day was around the corner, and I intended to capitalize on it.

I was overjoyed when the calls came inquiring about my offerings. I was even more excited when the calls turned from inquiry to actual orders, so I went to work to make it happen. I prepped the day before Mother's day as I was working alone and sorted out some of the smaller arrangements. I had to empty my refrigerator to accommodate the arrangements and even resorted to asking the neighbors to facilitate me with refrigerator space. The following morning, I was up at 4 am putting together the bigger arrangements; I was working like a ninja to make the morning deliveries.

It turned out to be a huge success; I had made my initial investment plus enough money to pay half my daughter's school fee as well as enough for the rent! Even though the business was seasonal, I made enough money to sustain us in off-seasons as I sold and delivered grapes, kiwis and plums. My chicken coup had rescued us!

I never took the business further but became acutely aware how some of us find our true calling or lifelong business in times of adversity. It became evident to me that nothing you do, no training you've ever received - informal or formal - is wasted. Adversity sharpened my business eye and gave me the added tenacity to get the job done. Today, I still remember and utilize the lessons learnt during those desperate times.

I want to acknowledge all the industrious mothers who have discovered their entrepreneurial spirit through the destitution of single parenting.

"Blessed are you who hunger now, for you shall be satisfied".

Worksheet No. 4

One of the biggest challenges for some single mothers is accessing enough financial resources to sufficiently meet their needs. If this is your situation please complete the following exercise.

1. List all of your skill sets.

2. Are you using any of these skills to make money now? If not, how can you start doing so?

3. Identify the resources you'd need to start utilizing one or more of your skill set (this includes finding a mentor or an investor)

4. Conduct a feasibility study and explore the options of turning your skill set into a business.

Chapter 10

Daddy Dearest

*"Any man can be a father, but it takes someone special to be
a dad"*

I have, on many occasions, stood at the window of my apartment and watched the father of my neighbor's children. I've watched him get the children in the mornings to go to school and observed him delivering grocerics to them every week. I've also seen him getting them for outings on the weekends and holidays. Both he and the mother appear to have an estranged relationship as their conversations never seem to go pass civil greetings. In-spite of this, nothing, from my vantage point, affects his interaction with his children.

I don't know his name, even though we exchange pleasantries, but I have so much respect for this man and his diligence regarding the care of his children. Admittedly, I used to feel a pinch of envy observing him then that slowly dissolved, as I became aware of my own blessings.

The First Meeting

My daughter met her father (for the very first time since she was 5 months old) on April 7, 2013. She was 8 years old.

In spite of his absence she was elated to hear that she would see him. She asked, "Mommy how long has it been since I've seen him?" Before I could answer her she said, "Oh yes, it's been 8 years."

I said, "Yes it has been".

She then said, "I am going to give him a big hug when I get there".

I asked, "What are you going to call him?"

She said, "I am going to call him Dad because he is my Dad".

Coming out of the conversation with my daughter, I was conflicted going into this meeting with her father. Janique was very excited, while I was very concerned. The "what ifs" kept playing over and over in my head. "What if he still wasn't ready to play an active role in her life?" "What if she connected with him and he vanished again?" I had always found solace in the fact that she wasn't old enough to witness our separation or to understand that he was consciously staying away from her, and I worried night and day that their meeting might impact her negatively. I took it to God in prayer and was then led to facilitate the meeting.

The meeting itself went well; but shortly after having met, he reverted to his old habits. Eight months went by before he asked to see her again. I was immensely grateful, however, that Janique was completely unperturbed by their interaction. I asked her how she felt and if she had any questions or concerns and she said she was just happy to have met him, period.

My Blessings

Sunday was father's day, and I received many father's day greetings from friends and family. I embraced them all with a smile as I've played dual roles since Janique was two months old. Evidently, the people in my village recognized this and made sure to acknowledge my efforts. I was grateful.

While this acknowledgement served to validate the roles I've always played in Janique's life, it didn't stop me from being pensive about the entire thing. When I sat in contemplation of my situation, I realized that even though her biological father had chosen to not be a part of her life, God had blessed her with some **POWERFUL FATHER FIGURES, who impacted her in one way or another**. At this time, I recognize the men who have played a significant role in my daughter's life.

VANCE DIEDRICK: This man is my father. He has been remarkable since Janique's birth. In those moments when I thought I would not have mentally made it, he, along with my mother, stepped in and kept Janique on weekends. He was

Janique's first father figure, and she knew it. As an infant, Janique would tell her friends who were inquiring about her dad that he was absent and proudly declare that she had an awesome grandfather. Thank you Dad.

KEVIN DAVE WALLEN: I am not certain where to start as it pertains to this GOD SENT. This magnificent man has been a part of Janique's life since her conception. He contributed to her welfare financially, psychologically and has made an indelible mark on her overall development over the years. Kevin carried her on his shoulders and held her in the water at the beach while she splashed around when she was younger. He consoled her when she was distressed and hugged her whenever they met. He taught her a butterfly kiss (batting eyelashes together) and attended her schools functions and took her to the movies with his son. He bought her gifts and held her hand when she was not in the mood to hold mine. He has loved and encouraged her. I thank you dearest Kevin, with everything that I am, for your role in my daughter's life.

CRAIG EDWARD FRANCIS: This gentleman has been a friend to me and an uncle to my child like no other. Craig took me to the supermarket when I had no money to buy groceries and contributed to Janique's school fee when I was unemployed. He came and got us when my car would not start, and on other occasions he took us on excursions or to his home to relax. He has been selfless and very supportive. Thank you Craig for your unwavering kindness.

My role as a single mother, thus far, has been very challenging; but in all things, God never left me. He gave me these amazing, beautiful souls to make the journey more bearable. May GOD'S RICHEST BLESSING OVERCOME YOU AWESOME MEN, AND THANKS AGAIN FOR BEING THERE FOR JANIQUE AND I. HAPPY, HAPPY FATHER'S DAY.

Worksheet No. 5

I am fully aware that no matter how a mother rises to the occasion to parent her child/children well, she can't replace the father. There are some important elements that only a man can bring to the parenting equation.

1. Does your child/children have a positive father figure or a male role model?

2. Do you think a male role model is necessary for your child/children? Explain.

3. What are the traits and personality characteristics you would want in a male role model if you don't currently have one? Get specific as you write out these attributes and make an effort to consciously pull this individual in your life.

Chapter 11

Owning My Stuff

"In every adversity lies the seed of an equal or greater opportunity." – Napoleon Hill

Philosophers and some of the great thinkers of our time have posited that we come into this world as blank slates and by virtue of our associations and experiences we begin the process of creating ourselves. These experiences have the power to make us bitter or better depending on how we perceive and internalize them.

I have spoken at length about the situation with my ex-husband. I talked extensively about the trials and triumphs of caring for my child, and I spoke about my first real love. All of these experiences shaped me and exponentially changed my outlook on life. In retrospect, I am a better person as a result of these unforeseen occurrences that tried, tested and molded me. Truth be told, I didn't always feel this way, but the lessons became clearer when I conscientiously made the decision to work on me.

Taking Responsibility

Things happen to everyone; it's a part of life's journey. But at some point, we must accept responsibility for the things we allow or things we attract by virtue of who we are. In order to do that, we must all be accountable and honest with whom we are.

The question I asked earlier still remains: "What manner of woman was I to have attracted this to my life?" "This" being a man who would opt to ignore his child.

To be completely honest, my ex-husband was not an accident but merely the manifestation of my predominant preoccupation around men at that time. It took me some time to face this harsh reality, since at first, it was hard for me to see that I was co-creating the look and the feel of my interaction with this man. On the surface, my ex-husband was the one with the major issues. He was the one suffering from depression, he was the liar and the cheating partner, and he was the absentee father. Armed with all these facts, it was easy to lay the horrendous happenings of our marriage squarely at his feet.

In 2010, after the heart wrenching loss of my most cherished relationship (first love), I decided it was time to start working on ME. Although I had been working as a life skills facilitator for a year at that point, my life was nowhere near what I wanted it to be. I felt awful as nothing seemed to be going right. I was unemployed, alone and broken. Something was clearly wrong with my formula because my two major relationships had all come undone at the seams, and I was the common denominator. What was I doing wrong? It was time to become the case study.

I started by examining my relationship template in an effort to establish my patterns. What kind of man was I attracting? I did an inventory of my major relationships. In my attempts to get a concise picture, I broke my template down into specific categories:

- I outlined how the relationships started.
- I looked at the hopes and expectations I brought into the relationships and what hopes I expected my partner to fulfil.

Other categories in no particular order included:

- Non-sexual (no penile penetration) or sexual interaction, personality traits/attitude.
- I looked at their world view and governing philosophy, self-concept, stage of life, familial connections/interactions.

The last things I dissected were:

- how the relationship ended and
- the role I played in that, then most importantly
- I looked at my first relationship with the first man in my life; I looked at my father.

Having categorized the issues, I uncovered some prevailing patterns and shocking similarities. As I increased the categories and deepened my analysis, the discoveries were mind-boggling. I had been seeing in my non-sexual relationships men who had little or no integrity, who lied and cheated. Interestingly, I quickly dismissed them and ran head first into the biggest liar and cheater I could encounter (my ex-husband). I had developed some fundamental thoughts around men that came from my earlier interactions that were so deeply entrenched in the subconscious level; so much so that it became my reality. Coming out of these encounters, I had for years, prior to meeting my ex-husband, focused on and talked at length about the kind of man I DID NOT want. By doing so, I manifested exactly that which I didn't want, because that was where I had placed all my attention and energy. In spite of my first love having some similarities to my ex-husband, he was the exception to the rule in many of the categories, especially when I reviewed how they impacted me and my personal growth. This wasn't enough to sustain our relationship, however, as we were in the throes of the battle with the demons of our past.

The picture that was created by this introspective exercise frightened me. It made me feel like a participant in one of the personal development workshops I facilitate. I was coming into the full awareness that my thoughts (fears, hurts and generational consciousness) had become things. I had given birth to the monsters in my head and nurtured them with as much care and attention as I had given to my own child. This realization was terrifying but somehow extremely empowering for me at the same time. It was a liberating reminder that I could change my outcome. It was apparent that I wasn't doomed to painful relationships if I (the one variable I could control) changed the way I viewed men. It was that simple… but God the work was HARD. There were so many layers that I needed to peel back, so many little things that required my attention in order to dissolve their power and influence, but I was determined that the work must be done.

I immersed myself in books, seminars, workshops and courses in a bid to increase my understanding of myself as well as to broaden my perspective on men and relationships. After a while, I could see clearly the role I played in some of the arguments with my ex-husband. I saw how I emasculated him with some of my comments and actions, and I saw where my fierce independence prevented him, at times, from playing his role. The pivotal moment came when I was able to see myself in the exchange with my first love, and how I had also cut him off in a similar fashion. I knew that accepting my role in the unpleasantness didn't diminish or justify what the men did, but I was now in a place to truly learn the lessons these encounters intended to teach ME about ME.

I started compiling notes on my findings and focused on how women, especially independent women, inadvertently sabotage themselves in their relations with men. This gave birth to my business <u>Fervida</u>, where I designed workshops to help women (through my own experiences and the work of others before me) navigate their relationships with themselves and the men in their lives.

No one could have told me that my experiences and owning my role in them would have been the genesis of the work I now do with women. Nevertheless, it served to reinforce something I tell my daughter when she is changing grades at school. I tell her that she doesn't get to choose her teacher; therefore, she won't get to negotiate the lesson plan, what will be taught or the length of time spent on any particular topic, neither will she have a say regarding how the lessons will be disseminated. I go on to tell her that she can only control how she will interact with her teacher and make the decision to learn what the teacher has to impart, regardless.

So many women find themselves in some very vicious cycles regarding their life choices. Most never stop to take stock of the part they're playing in this show and its multiple reruns as they focus primarily on the other actors and what they are doing or not doing to make them (the women) unhappy. Sadly, most never realize that the other actors are their teachers, and it is never about the teacher. Instead, it is always about you owning your stuff and choosing to be the student instead of the victim.

Worksheet No. 6

1. Draft your relationship template in the following categories:-

Start by listing your top 3 major relationships;

Next, write their names across a sheet of paper;

Place the following categories under each of the names

Category 1: Where did you meet?

Category 2: What did you want/expect from this person?

Category 3: Was the relationship sexual or non-sexual?

Category 4: List personality traits/ attitudes of each person.

Category 5: List their worldview/Life philosophy

Category 6: Self-concept

Category 7: character

Category 8: Stage of life

Category 9: Familial connections/interactions

Category 10: The way the relationship ended.

After filling in the categories for each person, identify the similarities and the differences. This template should reveal your relationship pattern (it should show the type of partners you have been attracting).

2. Once you have completed the category exercise, look at your relationship with your father, and list his personality traits, attitude, self-concept, character, worldview/philosophy.

Are there any similarities between your father/Guardian and your partner/s?

3. How did you contribute to the demise of your relationships? Explain

4. How did each of the relationship enhance you? Explain

Chapter 12

The Mothering Gene

No to the status quo

As a child growing up in the church, I used to believe that women became pregnant when they got married. I know it sounds ridiculous, but it was the only logical reason I could come up with as these happy, slender women would get married and within months of the marriage they began to swell in the waist line.

As I got older, I observed that the mothers had the physical responsibility of care for the children, even though the fathers were all present in church. The mothers would get help from the younger unmarried ladies who would take turns holding the infants but the care of the children rest predominantly with the women.

The same trend became apparent with my girlfriends when we all became mothers. On the weekends, we would get together to go the supermarket and carry the kids for ice cream or to some other recreational activity. I was the only single mother in the group, so my weekend activities had a little something extra. Janique was an early riser so on Saturdays I would take her to the pool by 9 am; we would be there for 3-4 hours. After that, I would take her home put her to bed and later meet up with the girls for the supermarket and ice cream run.

One day I was hanging out with two of my closest girlfriends, and I asked them how hands-on their husbands were with the children. One said her husband made an attempt to help as he would cook if she was preoccupied with the baby in the earlier stages and would occasionally take their child when she was older for weekends to his parents giving her some time to herself. The other said her husband spent time with their child on weekends when the helper was away and work had her out of town, but once she was home the child was mainly her responsibility.

I had other friends whose husbands spent long hours at work or just away from home and the onus was on the mothers to take care of the child in spite of all the other things they had to do. This was in direct contrast to what I had witnessed growing up. My father was very involved in our day to day care. He would keep us when my mother had errands to run. He made us breakfast most mornings and took us out most weekends. My mother never thought twice to leave us with him when she had to go overseas, and it was clear that he enjoyed this hands-on approach.

As a single mother, I understood that I would be the chief caregiver but I struggled to understand why my other married girlfriends found themselves in the same situation. I remember having a discussion with the husband of one of my girlfriends. I asked him why he didn't spend more time with his kids. He told me that he was the primary breadwinner and needed to work longer hours in order to sustain his family. He went on to say that on Saturdays he had to put in a few hours at work then get some recreational time in and on Sundays he rested for the upcoming week. I asked him if he realized how much of his children's lives he was missing out on and how this was impacting his wife. He admitted that he realized and would make an attempt to avail himself to them, so that his wife could get a much needed break.

I was thoroughly annoyed that this had to be a conversation. I have had similar conversations with some of the fathers I knew and was taken aback that most did not see their hands-off approach as an issue until we spoke. Maybe it was just me or maybe I didn't get enough of the maternal gumption that accepted this shit. Nevertheless, I wondered if these men were just emotionally inept in this regard or was it that over the years we, women, had done a poor job of conveying that we needed more help with the children. A part of me knew that I had become hypersensitive to women caring for their children on their own, but the other side felt that some fathers could do more. I understood the dynamics of the traditional role of the woman (nurturer and keeper of the home) and the man (provider and protector) but knew that this archetype had changed drastically in modern times. So many women, even those in marriages, have had to take up the position of provider and protector along with their other duties. I contemplated why in the face of this new reality some men still had a standoffish approach to caring for their children and why so many women perpetuated this cycle.

The Missing Link

Even though it is clear that my love for my child is like no other, I never felt having her was my defining moment. In fact, I often sat in silent wonderment when other mothers would openly gush about their children being their EVERYTHING and the reason they now LIVED and BREATHE. I could not relate and surmised that I might be missing some aspects of the mothering gene. I knew something changed in me from her conception, and it followed through to her birth as I became more protective, nurturing and tender. While patience and understanding also followed suit in her early childhood, I felt that maybe I might be missing something.

There was no question that my life was different when I became a mother, but I could not relate to some of the things some mothers said they felt. Having my daughter didn't bring any immense clarity on the direction my life would take. I didn't find renewed vigour for life and love and she was not my sole reason for living. I remember watching an interview with a young lady who became pregnant in university who broke down in tears saying she could not imagine her life without her daughter and that she was now living for her. I still remember my reaction to her comment, I scoffed at her, rolled my eyes and said, "Really now", as I had so many aspirations and things I intended to achieve that were independent of my child. I knew she would benefit and even influence some of my

decisions, but I never felt that she was now my reason for living. I simply did not identify with those echoed sentiments.
.

This is not to be mistaken with a lack of love, because I do love my child. Like many other mothers who wouldn't openly say, she did drive me crazy having had to deal with her all time. I looked forward to sending her to kindergarten/school and rejoiced from the mountain tops when my parents or girlfriends kept her. There were days I felt that if she said, "Mommy" one more time I would start screaming on the top of my lungs, and on many occasions I considered what my life would be like if I did not have the responsibility of caring for her. During the times when my frustration was through the roof, I felt like finding her father and saying, "Tag, you're it mother fucker! It's your time to keep her for the next couple of years; call me when she turns 16." Did this mean I wasn't a good mother? Surely, I was missing something as other mothers spoke with such conviction about the unceasing joy and the everlasting happiness their children brought them every day and how every breath they took now hinged on their blessing from God.

The entire experience of mothering challenged me on every level. it wasn't always joyful and fulfilling as some mothers portrayed it to be (clearly I came out of the shallow side of the maternal gene pool). As challenging as parenting/mothering was for me, the effects didn't stop there. I had come to resent being a single mother, and I felt gut-wrenching trepidation and disgust at the thought of having another child. I found it difficult to celebrate with friends/acquaintances that became pregnant in situations I deemed unsuitable (husbands cheating or absent most of the time or their relationship was new or generally unstable).   It became clear to me that I was projecting.

When I recognized the amount of negative emotions I had fostered for this, I started doing some work on myself. I managed to smooth off some of the rougher edges around the negative thoughts and made a conscious effort to constantly remind myself that *what you resist persists*. I started to pray and talk to others about it and even got to the place where I moved from being certain that I would never have another child to saying I would probably consider it if my next husband could afford a nanny that drove the kids around. The resentment I felt about being a single mother slowly waned, as I accepted my situation. Where the friends and other people were concerned, I rationalized that I didn't get to decide what was right or good for them. I finally accepted that it really was none of my business what they did with their lives (I had enough on my own plate).

I felt I had made some strides in the right direction until I had an episode when I went to visit a friend of mine in the hospital who had just given birth. I walked into the ward and became conscious of all the women there. Most were in bed with curtains half drawn and others were slowly walking in the aisles pulling along the mechanism with their intravenous lines. As I navigated the aisles, I saw more women in various state of discomfort caused by having given birth recently. The memory of my own harrowing experience came flooding back to me, and I felt overwhelmed. I started to wonder where the men were that impregnated these women; after all, it was visiting time. I wondered if they had support at home. I wondered if this was their first, second or third child and just felt very concerned for all of them.

On the way home I started to process my response and admitted that I still had work to do on myself. Single mothering had left very deep and long scars in my core that still existed even though I was conscientious in my efforts to renew my mind. I reminded myself that emotional scarring had many levels that could affect different aspects of one's life; therefore, I needed to be gentle with myself. I reminded myself that based on the depth of the emotional scarring, each level could surface at different times. Then I reminded myself that in spite of everything, I was still a great mother; my daughter told me so.

Worksheet No. 7

94

Make short notes on the following, and then read them aloud to yourself:

1. How has being a single mom impacted you and your views towards parenting?

2. How has single motherhood affected your relationship with your child/children?

Chapter 13

To New Beginnings

It is interesting to witness how the little things that take place in our lives can serve as a catalyst for new beginnings. My life was not short of events that became the catalyst for change, and my experience of being Janique's mom provided just that. It had been three weeks and counting since my daughter Janique quit sucking her thumb, and I was elated as we had been locked in an ongoing battle over said finger for the last 8 years.

When I took Janique home from the hospital she weighed 5lbs 5oz, and none of the things I had purchased for her fit. One such purchase was her pacifiers. I had gotten at least 6 of them and all were too big for her tiny mouth. This was a source of concern for me, as I noticed her tendency to put her hands in her mouth when she got hungry or was about to go to sleep. I had spoken to her pediatrician about an alternative to the pacifier but he told me not to worry because if she did not latch on to the pacifier it was perfectly fine for her to suck her thumb.

I was far from amused with his comments, so I employed my own measures to keep her hand and fingers out of her mouth. I made numerous attempts to get her accustomed to the pacifier, but that didn't work. The fingers kept going to her mouth with greater regularity, so I put socks on her hands. That lasted for about two weeks when I felt she had forgotten about the fingers. To my surprise as soon as it was time to sleep she would start to suck her thumb. I started putting the sock only on the hand with the finger she favored, and she resorted to sucking the thumb on the other hand.

I finally stopped using the socks, and by the time she was 4 months the sucking of the thumb became a permanent fixture. As she got older, she started to suck her thumb while she caressed whatever soft cloth or clothing she could find. I was perturbed for a while, as I too sucked my thumb as a child (caressing soft clothing as well) and managed to muster the courage to quit on the eve of my 13th birthday, so I was worried that she might follow suit.

As she grew older, my father and I employed all kinds of tactics to force her to quit. When she was younger, my father used to apply the slimy juice from the Aloe Vera plant to her finger (which is a very bitter taste) but she would wash off the offensive substance, and it was business as usual. When she got older, I spoke to her about how thumb-sucking could affect the alignment of her teeth and showed her pictures of children with various stages of misaligned teeth. That prompted an attempt on her part to stop at 7 years old. This did not last; she threw in the towel after a week.

I decided to change my strategy as the scare tactics hadn't yielded any lasting results. It was time to reason with her about her addiction, so I explained to her what was really happening the best way I could. I told her that sucking her thumb was what she used to calm and comfort herself, and the feeling of the soft clothing was just an extension of the way she relaxed. I went on to explain that she had developed an association with sucking her finger and feeling the soft piece of clothing. She listened keenly, as I spoke and I gave her examples as I expounded my theory. I went on to explain that she was selective in her decision to suck her thumb as she did not do so at school or in the presence of her friends. This being the case, it was clear she could break the habit quicker than she thought.

She took my advice and embarked on another quest to free herself of the finger. About three days into this trial, we were watching the television and she said, "Mommy I really want to stop sucking my finger but my mind is telling me to put it in my mouth."

I said, "Very good observation. The mind is doing its job of reminding the body that we are relaxing and it is finger sucking time. You have to resist the temptation to suck your thumb until your body no longer wants it as much." I went on to tell her that it would be difficult in the first week but that things would get a little easier with each passing day. I felt we were making good progress, until she hit a rut and went back into full remission after a week and half.

The Game Changer

The week before Janique's 10th birthday, I revisited the conversation about her quitting the thumb sucking. She had many excuses as to why this was next to impossible unless she got some professional help. She had told me that her best friend at school had gotten a program from a doctor that helped her to stop sucking her fingers, so she felt she needed to visit this doctor to finally sort herself out. I, on the other hand, believed she could do it if she set her mind to it. Unfortunately, as more time went by and her habit persisted, I started to feel that we might need the help of the good doctor after all.

The Catalyst For Janique's Change

We were in the second week of July and I bought her another book in the series of *Diary of a Wimpy Kid (The Ugly Truth),* which is her all-time favorite set of books. Now one afternoon whilst reading the book she asked me, "What is a headgear?" I asked her what she was talking about and she showed me a picture of a child wearing a headgear for his braces. I explained that it was an addition to his braces to help his teeth align themselves. She fell silent and started reading again. I went back to doing what I was on my computer; shortly after, I heard her sobbing. I looked up and asked her what was wrong and when she turned to face me, tears were streaming down her face. She then said, trying hard to control her sobbing, that she didn't want to have to wear a headgear if she needed to get braces. I was speechless as she continued her outpouring. She wept as she told me how embarrassed she would be if she had to wear a headgear to school and how the kids would say unkind things to her. I asked her why she felt she would need braces and a headgear. Then I asked her why she was she was making these heavy predictions about her future.

After I managed to calm her, I then told her how I quit sucking my thumb. It was the week of my 13th birthday and the realization hit me that I was going to be a teenager and was still sucking my thumb in spite of all the tactics my family used over the years to force me to break the habit. I went on to tell her that the thought of becoming a teenager with what I considered to be a childish practice was enough for me to make the decision to stop once and for all. I did it in one week, and I told her how difficult it was when I just started and used to fall asleep with the thumb under my pillow to ensure that I did not put it in my mouth, but I did it.

She then said, "If you did it, so can I." On the same day, July 8th 2014 she started her journey becoming more deliberate than the times before to overcome her finger.

I told her to cross out each day on the calendar that she did not put the finger in her mouth and this would be a reminder that she was quitting a day at a time. One week went by, and she handled herself like a champ. However, three days into the second week she started telling me that she was feeling for her finger. This would happen in the evenings when we were both relaxing over a movie or book. When it happened, I would remind her why she was feeling the urges so strongly. We would talk it through, and she would be alright. On the fourth night of the second week, Janique readied herself for bed and had a meltdown. She called me into the room and told me she was going out of her mind with how badly she wanted to suck her finger. He eyes were wild and she complained that she was having a headache as she ran her hands vigorously through her hair. I explained that this was a part of the process and that the mind/body was only sending more intense nudges that it wanted what it had become accustomed to. It took her a long time to fall asleep. She tossed and turned repeatedly, hissed her teeth then finally buried her head under the pillow leaving her thumb out.

As I watched her that night I was reminded of people going through rehabilitation to quit their addictions in a bid to bring back some semblance of normalcy to their lives. I witnessed my daughter struggle to break a habit she had fostered for the last eight years, and I knew her struggle, pain and discomfort were real. Two big drops of tears fell from her eyes before she covered her head under the pillow, and I prayed for her. I thought of all the people (myself included) who, at some point in life, embarked on the journey to break their self-defeating habits. For some, it was trying to resist the clutches of negative thoughts, past hurts and fears and for others, it was breaking the insanity of choosing the same kind of poison that masqueraded as lifestyle, lovers and friendships. I considered how so many failed time and time again in their attempt to free themselves of these addictions and patterns that became their default setting.

Progress marker

The next day I asked her how she felt and she said, "Last night was horrible Mommy. I felt like I was going out of my mind if I didn't get to suck my finger."

I asked her, "Did you go out of your mind?" She said, "Yep." I said, "Very Good! When you are out of mind you are in spirit and that is when you connect to God and find peace."

She said, "Great! I feel a lot better today."

I told her to get the marker and x out another day on her journey to freedom. She jumped off the bed in glee with marker in hand and she was smiling from ear to ear when she shouted, "Goodbye finger. Hello GOOD LIFE."

I laughed with her and told her how proud I was that she had persevered and gave her a high five then reminded her that she could accomplish anything she wanted once she applied herself and stuck to her commitment one day at a time.

Some profound lessen stood out for me in all this:

1. As a transformational coach, I tell people asking if I can "fix them" that it isn't my job to do so. I go on to say that I can only facilitate that process as no matter how insightful the advice they get out of our sessions they have to make the decision to change and sustain the commitment to apply the information given to their daily lives.

2. Nothing beats the power of a made up mind. We can achieve what we once considered to be impossible when the decision is made to get it done.

3. Old habits die hard, but our evolution and the ultimate manifestation of the best version of ourselves lie on the other side of the things that make us uncomfortable.

Addictions and patterns have so many people chasing their tails, and sadly very few manage to stay the course necessary to change their lives even after seeing the cycle they are caught up in and how it limits their growth. I was happy that my daughter understood that dropping this habit had greater implications around the character she was building and ultimately the person she was becoming because she persevered through the tough times, faced her fears, stayed true to her commitment and challenged herself to raise the bar for her life. Cheers my sweet child. Let us raise our glasses to greater possibilities and new beginnings.

Worksheet No. 8

1. Have you identified your self-defeating habits? List them and write about how they have impacted or continue to impact your life.

2. Have you taken any steps to rid yourself of these habits? Write about the measures you've employed.

3. If you haven't done anything yet or you failed in your attempt/s to get over these habits, are you prepared to try something new to finally free yourself?

4. Write about this new method you're prepared to try. Outline what are the steps you will take to get and utilize this new method then put a time line to your intentions.

Chapter 14

The Noon Day Demon

I explained earlier the many challenges I experienced with being married to a Manic Depressive man. Having heard about the late actor, Robin Williams' battle as a manic depressive and his ultimate suicide, I felt compelled to talk a little more about my encounter with this dreadful demon, depression.

Andrew Solomon the author of **The Noon Day Demon: An Atlas of Depression** (one of the best books I've read on the subject), writes aptly about depression. He states that "depression is the flaw in love. To be creatures who love, we must be creatures who can despair. When it comes, it degrades oneself and ultimately eclipses the capacity to give or receive affection. It is the aloneness within us made manifest and it destroys not only connection to others but also the ability to be peacefully alone with oneself".

I don't know if the average mind can comprehend depression. Personally, I struggled to wrap my brain around it.

What I know for sure is that pain is a part of the human experience. Since this is an undeniable fact, we will feel sadness at some point in our lives brought on by some unexpected or expected event. In this form, we are predisposed to many shifts in our moods that can lead to feelings of despair, desolation and despondency. While I was very aware of this, nothing prepared me for the measureless pain linked to my ex-husband's existence. From my vantage point, it was an unspeakable horror. His depression manifested itself in a number of ways. The first sign I detected was how erratic his moods were. We would be out having a good time, and he would suddenly become withdrawn. When I enquired what was wrong, he would reply that he needed to leave. At other times, his restlessness could only be sated with fishing or sex. I remember making several weekend trips with him to Port Royal, Portmore and Ocho Rios to throw out a line. Fishing calmed him down considerably and almost always put him in a good mood. It brought out his patient side, and I would watch him sit by the seashore wrapping fishing line unto a reel and attaching different pound weights and baits.

Where sex was concerned, he had quite an appetite. Although I didn't know this at the time he had utilized sex as a means of staving off the all-powerful grip of his depression. I believe that the dopamine release and the heightened serotonin levels triggered by an orgasm, fed his addiction to sex. Our sexual exploits were proof of that as were his many, many other encounters with the women that serviced his insatiable appetite during our marriage.

The other thing that blind-sided me during our marriage was the debilitating effects of his condition when he was depressed. He would move from being active in the gym, at work and school to literally having very little engagement in anything at all. His depressive episodes were nothing short of an alien invasion. He became a sliver of his former jovial, playful and productive self on his birthday in March; and for the next 9 months, "the apparition" possessed him. Firstly, he lost his appetite for food. He went from 7 square meals a day to a patty and drinks. His weight loss was always so dramatic, as his 200 pound muscle bound frame would wither away in less than a month. I recall vividly trying feverishly to feed him soup in the evenings as he laid curled in a fetal position. He had lost all interest - and I mean all interest - in most of his favourite pastime. It became a monumental task for him to get out of bed in the mornings.

His depression also manifested in forms of rage. I recall vividly the many pointless arguments that were a fixture of our marriage as well as the times I saw his rage spring forth. In one argument, we were face to face, toe to toe going at it and in one swift movement he turned away from me and drove his fist and forearm through the bathroom door. I didn't flinch and neither did he; but when he turned to look at me, his eyes were unrecognizable. It was as if a beast was awakened in him, and it took everything in me to hold his gaze and stand my ground. He never hit me during our time together, but toiletries got swept off the dressers and pots got knocked off the stove on quite a few occasions.

Solomon (author of Noon Day Demon), after recounting his moments of rage said, "I felt as though I were disappearing, and somewhere deep in the most primitive part of my brain, I felt that violence was the only way I could keep myself and mind in the world". This resonated with me, and there was a side of me that wondered if this was the fight my ex-husband faced when the rage overcame him.

In the beginning none of this made sense to me, because on the surface he appeared normal.   My mind struggled to comprehend how this seemingly healthy, well-thinking man couldn't find the will power to even brush his teeth. I recall asking him to explain what he was experiencing, and he said he felt weighted down coupled with an overpowering sadness that was incapacitating. He said everything, even the idea of a smile, seemed so painfully difficult at times. He went on to say that there were times he felt hungry but couldn't find the will to eat and eventually the hunger just faded into the background as the listlessness consumed him. He said he just wanted to lie down as if he had fallen and couldn't get up.

My heart broke more and more each year as I realized the magnitude of his affliction. The more I edified myself on the condition, the more frightened I became because none of the medication guaranteed a full recovery. Added to this was the fact that the side effects of the medication seemed worse than the condition it was intended to treat, and it didn't help either that they were extremely costly. As we made the rounds from psychiatrist to psychiatrist - over and over - we were told that there were no guarantees with the medication; it was really a trial and error situation. It was difficult for me to watch, and I remember him complaining bitterly about some of the side effects. Some gave him dry mouth, and there was one in particular that made him sleepy. He told me that he would pull up to the stop light and fall asleep behind the steering wheel or he would be in between sets of lifting weights at the gym and was overcome with sleep. Another drug affected his erection (he stopped that one immediately). The drugs with the exception of one that really worked for him (*Motival*) had him in a bigger tail spin, and I would watch helplessly as he juggled the act of staying afloat on drugs that at best made flimsy swings at the demon whose all-encompassing grip was so crippling.

"That life is worth living is the most necessary of assumptions". George Santayana

He became suicidal when he started taking Lithium.

Two years had gone by with multiple attempts to immobilize the effects of the demon with a plethora of drugs. We were both frustrated as our lives were spiraling out of control. One minute he was employed and seemed poised to make great strides, and the next he could not function on the job and was fired. He went through 7 jobs in 3 ½ years. Then there was the ongoing drama with school. He enrolled in university a total of three times and had to discontinue because he just could not cope when the depression reared its ugly head. I was living a life of quiet desperation, as I kept the reality of his condition secret from my friends and family out of fear they wouldn't understand and would judge him. I suffered in silence and it chipped away at me for years.

He had stopped taking the medication for a few months and fell into a really bad slump and was prescribed *Lithium* along with two other drugs. I was very attentive when he started new drugs and read everything I could on them to stay abreast. I knew something was off when he started to lose sleep. He said it was taking him longer to fall asleep and because the sleep wasn't restful he would get up in the middle of night and would be awake for hours. Then came what I refer to as the *'fatalistic talk'*. For the very first time, he started talking about how awful he felt and how his life had amounted to nothing. I knew that depression feed invalidation as it seem to reside in that place that all of us as humans visit periodically; that place which houses our fears and insecurities and amplifies our perception of worthlessness. My ex became progressively saddened over his state of affairs and would remain almost catatonic in the bed on weekends. Not even the suggestion of going fishing could get him to move.

One day while feeding him in bed he told me he had had enough. He said he felt like he couldn't go on any more and that nothing seemed to shake the feeling that it was time to end his futile existence. His eyes were hollow and broken; the skin on his face was blotchy and his weight was down to 165 pounds. He looked emaciated lying there and the gravity of his words hit me like a freight train. I knew in that moment that he was prepared to end his life. Nothing could explain the range of emotions that engulfed me, and I did the only thing I felt I could do. I called his father who was, ironically, a Psychiatrist and told him that I was coming over. I helped my ex-husband get ready then I secured his fire arm and license in my hand bag and drove like a bat out of hell to his parent's home. When we got there I spoke to his father alone and totally lost all self-control as I shed rivers of tears I had held in place just to be strong for him during his battle with this force that seem so impenetrable. I gave his Dad his gun and told him I thought he needed to stay with them for a while until this phase passed as I had to be at work in the days. He facilitated me and kept his son for week and changed his medication.

I visited him after work for the week he was with his parents and took him home on the weekend. Thankfully, the change of medication lifted his mood and that was the last of the suicidal talk.

*The late Robin Williams, comedienne and Actor On August 11, 2014, committed **suicide** at age 63, allegedly because of issues relating to depression.*

Having had to co-exist with someone with depression was a journey into the bowels of hell and back. I prayed unceasingly for a breakthrough as I witnessed first-hand the uncontrollable and incomprehensive suffering my ex-husband faced during our time together. Being a prisoner of your mind as a result of your physiological make up is a burden that no one should have to bear for a protracted period of time in a world where the majority can only relate to a particular concept of normality.

I believe the world, especially in my neck of the woods (Jamaica), need to embark on a public education campaign on depression/mental health disorders and its effects and treatment in teenagers, adults and the elderly. I find it appalling that a condition that is so pervasive in our society and the world over only gets the spotlight when someone notable or otherwise decides to take matters into his/her own hands and end their life. The truth of the matter is that depression and other mental health disorders are very real and formidable opponents, and I say so only from my position as an observer. I implore us who wake up in the mornings with the will to live and do and make our mark to be mindful, kind and gentle to another who we have labeled bitchy, stand offish/snobbish, miserable, mean-spirited or unkind on the bases of their behavior. You can never really know the personal monsters these people are wrestling with.

My prayers and heart go out to the family of Robin Williams in their moment of grief and all others among us who continue to suffer in silence with this demon called Depression.

Mirth

Chapter 15

Forty and Fabulous

Today I'm forty years old and as I sit in quiet contemplation I am aware that subconsciously I've made this day, this time, into a major milestone. I understand the human need to set timelines for our lives as a means of gauging our accomplishments which we use to assess our personal success. Still, I am uncertain when I mentally made this age - this specific number - a milestone.

I remember consciously making my 25th birthday a major marker to assess the achievement of my academic goals. I had secured my first degree in business by this time but my plans had to change mid-stream, as I became saturated with what had been my focus for the last 5 years and made the shift into another area - Psychology. I remember being really sad for my 25th birthday because my life events weren't unfolding the way I had intended. This change of focus wasn't in my life forecast, and I was despondent because my picture perfect plan now had an unexpected turn; this made my idealistic mind scream "MAYDAY"!!! "MAYDAY"!!! Looking back now, I think this first real glitch in my matrix was setting the stage for the many others that would follow suit as my life unfolded.

As I bring my attention to this number 40, I realize the power of information and how it impacts us (which is partially why the number is subconsciously important to me). According to society, the woman at forty should be "settled". What exactly does that mean? Well, that means she should be well established in her career; she should be married with the two and half kids; she should have the house (which her husband bought) with the white picket fence and the BMW in the driveway. The idea of being 40 (especially for females) is something the world has placed a great deal of emphasis on. The forty year old woman has had her entire life mapped out for her in terms of what she should have achieved at this age. How we should be living and what we should have acquired by this time are all spelled out in all the popular magazines. It's highly touted in most movies and by extension we have unknowingly taken these ideals unto ourselves.

Woe be unto the poor forty year old female who finds herself lacking in any of the above-mentioned departments when this ALL IMPORTANT birthday comes around. I have worked with women who've become depressed because they don't have the husband, child(ren), the multiple degrees or the house and car. I've seen what so many of these ladies resort to when they believe that time is running out. I've witnessed women marry men locally and abroad whom they barely know, let alone love, just because it's time to "settle down". Others have married men for the things the men have accomplished, while others literally become pregnant for any man because the age forty is quickly approaching.

I am elated at this stage of my life that while some of society's dictates have impacted me and may have been the driving force behind some of my earlier decisions, I've managed to set my own life markers and chart my own path. This doesn't mean that I've never compared myself to another and felt that I've been wasting precious time. There are still some things that I am yet to do; I am yet to purchase my first home. Added to that, my marriage ended in divorce. Had I continued on the career path of business (I was once a superb and successful sales manager), I'm certain I would have been a prominent player in the field by now. In spite of this, I'm eternally grateful, at this moment, for my accomplishments and above all else, I'm grateful for the person I've become.

Everything I have been through, good or bad, has provided me with some of my greatest achievements – tangible or intangible. Even though my first marriage failed, our union produced my beautiful daughter, Janique. I changed my career path to become a transformational coach; and in spite of the many setbacks and the days and nights in tears and prayers over the uncertainty of my present business, <u>Fervida</u>, I know, beyond a shadow of a doubt, that this is my calling. My personal growth and evolution has been monumental. I've seen the many sides of life from my personal experiences or vicariously through the eyes of those I've come into contact through work or otherwise.

Because of the experiences I have had, I've lost the plethora of judgments I had in my twenties after life brought them all to my door step. One by one, I was able see the ugliness I so readily pointed out in others in myself. For the judgments that persisted, I've worked diligently to bring the higher vibrations of love and understanding to the picture. I have also been able to release the people that I no longer need to be in my life with grace and love. I've forgiven myself for the mistakes I've made and incorporated the lessons learnt in my life and in my work with women. I've forgiven the people who hurt me. I've survived some major battles and healed what was broken. Most importantly, I have learnt to love unconditionally and whole-heartedly in spite of my fierce desire to protect myself. Despite my previous preoccupation with planning and seeing every step clearly. I've learnt, above all else, to surrender, and to let go and to let God.

Today I'm 40 years old and I'm even more AMAZING, SPECTACULAR AND FABULOUS than I've ever been. My best days are here!!

Chapter 16

Happy Birthday Baby

Janique waiting for me to get ready

Today is my daughter's 10th birthday, and I'm elated. This journey as a mother has been quite the experience. I've grown in leaps and bounds over the last 10 years primarily because of the many unforeseen ups and down in my role as mother. Now, I look back and feel a sense of great accomplishment. My daughter, at 10, is a bright, securely attached child; she's forthright and honest. She is kind and makes an attempt to be fair in her dealings with her peers; and more than anything else, she is a lover of life.

Although I am not a helicopter mom nor am I one of those mothers whose world begins and ends with their child, my daughter's presence has been somewhat of a stabilizing force for me; and she has opened aspects of me that only unconditional love could unlock.

In my line of work I've seen, in no uncertain terms, the impact parents have on their children, both positively and negatively. As a result, I've spent a great deal of time fixing me, cleaning up my karma and making the necessary adjustments in my personality to give her the best possible chance to navigate the bumps on the road of life that she might face because of my dysfunction. She's made me a better person and a better mother.

Giving Thanks

I contracted the awful virus Chikungunya about 2 months prior to my daughter's 10th birthday, and was laid up in bed bawling over the incapacitating effects of this wretched virus. I started thinking about the people that only God could have sent to aid me as I journeyed with my child Janique. Earlier, I thanked the men that fathered Janique and today on her birthday, I salute the following ladies who showed me kindness and played just as important a role in raising her:

- The first woman that comes to mind is my mother, ***Gloria Diedrick***, for keeping Janique when I needed a moment to myself or had business to attend to. This simple act over the years kept me sane. To her, I am forever grateful.

- Special thanks to ***Dion Law*** who, on so many occasions (especially when Janique was younger), would call me to say that she's taking Janique for the weekend. Janique and Dion's daughter Alex have been friends since birth and being at Dion's home gave Janique an opportunity to experience the feel of having siblings. According to Janique, Auntie Dion is the epitome of the "activity mom" as such time spent at her home was always a blast; Dion had them playing in the dirt, driving go carts, playing the Wii. She had them making pizza, hot dog, baking brownies and cookies or doing just about anything, within reason, that kept them active. Thank you, Dion, for the role you have played and for treating my child as you do your own. May you continue to be blessed in everything you do.

- I am very grateful for ***Kisha Bailey and Tamara Mitchell*** for being there for Janique and I when things became financially difficult. Both ladies reside overseas and made it their point of duty to call me during my unemployment to ask what Janique needed. They sent her clothes and school supplies on many occasions which took some of the financial pressure off me. Thank you both for your kindness.

- Lastly, I must mention ***Josette La Hee***. This God-sent has been a silent force in the life of my child. Her unwavering concern and kindness fills me with much gratitude. Thank you.

Part II

Chapter 17

Spear The Rod And Spoil The Child

If ever there was a tangible justification for birth control, I can safely say that my neighbor's child is the epitome of that. Never, in all my life, had I seen so much temper tantrums and hissy fits. It's ridiculous, to say the least. Each time I observe this child holding the entire family at ransom with her behavior, I'm reminded why I'm grateful for my child and why I'm certain one child is more than enough for me.

When I was growing up, there were many things my parents didn't tolerate. The first thing on that list was what my parents referred to as unruly behavior. My mother kept us all in check with just one stare. This "one stare" came into play, for the most part, at church. We would be in the middle of a very long church service and decide to start playing with one of the children sitting beside us or behind us as the case might be. The playing would start out subtly such as sharing a joke, but this would escalate into more talking, snickering and loud laughter. My mother would then turn around in her seat to check if my sister and I were the source of the disturbance. Once she confirmed that, we would get the intense "I'm going to break your bones" stare. That stare was usually all it took to end the fun and bring our attention back to the sermon.

I remember taking my daughter to the doctor for a check-up when she was just a few weeks old. The doctor was a young bright and bubbly mother of two children and whilst examining Janique she asked if she was my first child, and I said yes. She stopped what she was doing and said, "Get her used to your environment, if you're noisy get her use to that, allow her to fall into your routine". Her advice became a guiding force in my parenting style, as I was determined to amalgamate Janique into my life in a way that wasn't too stressful. I had seen my girlfriends struggling to get back to some kind of normalcy after they had gotten their children accustomed to sleeping in their beds, eating certain foods and tolerating undesirable behavior. I saw how so many of us, without realizing it, turned our children into little monsters simply because we facilitated behaviors that we thought were cute and adorable, until it became the bane of our existence.

As a teenager, I went into a store and heard a child demanding his mother to purchase a toy. She told him she wasn't going to get it, and he started insisting that he should have it. She continued to say no, but this was met with a loud scream. They instantly became the focal point of everyone in the store. The mother, clearly feeling embarrassed, made a bold attempt at being stern in order to rein in the child. He looked her straight in the eye and raised his voice at least three more octaves and started jumping then he threw himself to the floor. My left eye started twitching, and I swore I was about to pop a blood vessel watching the fiasco unfold. She stood over him visibly flustered and perturbed calling his name; he wouldn't budge and only screamed louder. My mother came to mind, as I envisioned what she would have done to me or any one of my siblings if we had a lapse in sanity and started acting out like this when we were younger. Let's just say there would have been hell to pay. I overheard other women in the store chiding the mother because of her inability to get the child under control, in that moment I promised myself that if ever I had children, that they would have to be disciplined from home to prevent this kind of public fracas.

I know very well that it's no walk in the park to raise a child, and by no means am I suggesting that I have mastered the art of raising a well-rounded and functional individual. What I do know is the importance of establishing healthy routines and setting boundaries. Like us, babies are creatures of habit; hence, we can condition them in ways that lead to a more harmonious existence for all concerned. Having said that, I'm fully aware that our little bundles of joy have different temperaments, so a cookie-cutter approach would not have worked. The following are some of the measures I have put in place to ensure my sanity and my daughter's safety.

- <u>Breast feeding</u>: In the second trimester of my pregnancy, my mother had a talk with me. She spoke about the importance of breast feeding my child but reminded me that it was necessary to have a reasonable weaning point. Reasonable for her was when baby turned 3 months. Her explanation was that I would want my body back - breasts and all – so it was wise for me to handle the whole business of feeding baby. I am aware that this conversation about breastfeeding is a sensitive one, especially in light of the backlash some mothers experience in some countries when publicly breast feeding, but it's worth taking a look at.

I made the decision to breast feed Jan exclusively in the first month of life because she came prematurely but started to supplement her feedings with baby formula. It was important to me to be able to pop a bottle in her mouth if I wasn't in the mood to breast feed or if I needed to leave her with someone. I used to express milk as well but noticed that when I gave her the formula just before bedtime at night she slept for longer hours and only woke up once in the night to be fed. This afforded me some more sleep and peace of mind in the event I needed to be away from her. I had/have girlfriends who breastfed exclusively and their children have become hand bags, so they can't leave them with anyone. Now, I understand that "the breast is best," but I feel it's necessary to create some balance, especially as a single mother. Breast feeding is an awesome way for a mother to bond with her baby, but I've heard women complaining about not having a life as they always have to be with their child due to breastfeeding exclusively. Others complain about sagging breast when they choose to breast feed the child for 2 years and more. I weaned Janique at almost 4 months old, and it served me well as it created balance.

- <u>Sleeping habits</u>: The pediatrician I talked about earlier had also told me that her babies slept in another room as soon as they came home from the hospital. I took a cue from that conversation, and whilst I wasn't comfortable with my daughter sleeping in another room, I ensured that she got used to sleeping in the basinet at the end of my bed as soon as I brought her home from the hospital. Culturing this habit saved my life. Because I allowed her to stay in the basinet when she woke up in the mornings, she learned how to entertain herself. This gave me time to get a bottle ready and use the bathroom in relative peace (priceless and simple pleasures as a single mother). Once she was fed, then it was bonding time. I would take her for a nature walk then it was play time (lots of singing and romping) I would give her a bathe then another feeding if necessary. Sleep would usually follow suit, and I would promptly put her back into the basinet. The only time Janique slept in my bed was when she was stuffy (nasal congestion from a cold) or griping,in which case we both slept topless with her on my chest.

When Janique was a toddler, I maintained a routine with her. Once she had dinner, I gave her water, brush her teeth and allowed her to play for an hour then it was reading time in preparation for bed at 8 p.m each night. I never got in bed with her in order to make her fall asleep. That was just not something I neither encouraged nor did. My girlfriends used to marvel at her ability to just hop in bed and fall asleep after we said prayers. It was shocking to them as they had to lie in their child's bed for them to fall asleep or the child only slept in their bed. They all complained about not getting enough time for themselves as their child/children were constantly up waiting on them to go sleep or that it was difficult to bond with their husbands as the child/children slept between them. Some of them had challenges leaving the child with babysitters as they would be restless and wouldn't sleep until mommy or daddy came home.

- <u>Disciplinary action</u>: Since I adopted some of the disciplinary measures from my parents, there was a zero tolerance for anything that resembled "unruly behaviour". There was considerably less infractions that fell under this category for me than it did for my parents, but there were some things I adhered to. The parameters were set from early, and I had no time or space for temper tantrums. Janique came to quickly understand that no amount of wailing would get me to bend to her way when she was acting out and "the look" stopped her in her tracks. I made it clear that certain behaviors were unacceptable; hence, she grew up knowing how to conduct herself in certain settings. As parents, we must recognize that we are the adults; we brought our children into the world and exposed them to what they have seen and experienced. With this in mind, we have the power to bring them up and train them in ways that help to make them manageable and functional.

Parenting is ridiculously hard work, and how we as parents manage the various stages our children go through is impacted by the elements such as our childhood, our parents and our life experiences. I believe we can make things easier for ourselves, however, if we (mothers) recognize that motherhood isn't martyrdom. We can groom our child/children in a way that gives us reasonable amounts of freedom to breathe and pursue our dreams. Our children weren't meant to dictate every aspect of our lives but to enhance it; therefore, we must create balance, so we can all thrive.

Worksheet No. 9

1. Have you been raising your child/children in a way that helps to create and maintain balance for all of you? Write about the things you've been doing in this regard.

2. If you find that there is little balance with the way you've been raising your child identify what adjustments you think you need to make to create a more harmonious situation?

Chapter 18

Lay Down Your Burdens

I remember a song we use to sing at church when I was a child. It says:
> "I'm gonna lay down my burdens, down by the riverside (down by),
> Down by the riverside (down by), down by the riverside.
> I gonna lay down my burdens, down by (down by the river side),
> I ain't gonna study war no more."

The message that the first part of the song conveyed was very clear to me even though I was yet to identify the relevance of the "Ain't gonna study war no more" part.

Janique and I had just finished one of our invigorating talks and I was sending her to bed. She then said, "Mommy, I have something to tell you."

I said, "Go ahead" noticing that she was somewhat hesitant.

She said, "You have to promise not to tell Grandpa."

I said, "I can't make any promises just yet, I need to know what we're dealing with."

She laid on the ground staring into the ceiling trying to muster up the courage to tell me what was on her mind then she started talking.

She told me about her visit with the grandparent's (my parents) over the weekend and playing with the chickens which was a part of her routine there. She said Grandpa asked her to give the chickens some water which she did. Tears were welling up in her eyes as she went on to explain that after filling up the water pan she continued to play with one of chickens. She said it started drinking water and she held its head in the pan for a second and it stop moving. At this point she was crying.

I paused for a few minutes before I said anything and just allowed her to cry. Then I asked her why she hadn't said it to me earlier. She said she didn't have the guts to say it to me the day she came home, but she kept thinking about the incident and felt she had to talk about it. She said when it happened she asked Grandpa to take her home immediately. She went on to explain that she wanted to tell my parents helper, but decided against it as she felt she would have told Grandpa and she was fearful of the repercussions. More tears came and then I told her to give me a high five; she looked at me confused and asked me what for. I told her that it took courage to tell me what she had done and by virtue of telling me it would alleviate some of the guilt she was feeling and that would take it out of her mind eventually.

She sat up and said, "Mommy the guilt isn't in my mind, it is in my heart."

With more tears flowing she covered her face and said, "I killed something." I said, "Yes, you did, however, let us look at the lessons here."

Janique has always been a lover of animals and birds as such I knew beyond a shadow of a doubt that she didn't intend to hurt the chicken. With this in mind I told her how important it was to be very careful when playing with animals and with her peers as accidents do happen.

I told her how much I appreciated the fact that she felt she could tell me this in spite of her fear of an unfavorable response. I then reiterated how courageous she was to have said it to me and used the opportunity to reinforce the importance of always telling me the truth as I can only offer assistance and guidance when I know the truth. I told her that the guilt she felt would soon pass, however, it was more important for her to focus on what the experience was meant to teach her. We hugged and I sent her to get ready for bed.

After our discussion, the song I mentioned earlier, came to mind forcefully. I have often wondered if I have done or said anything to Janique that affected her negatively. I'm talking about that one thing or series of events a person witnesses or experience as a child with their parents, family, peers or strangers that forever changed the way they view life and love. As it pertains to the negative, I feel that my being miserable, shouting occasionally or according to Janique not being more of an activity mom might have struck a nerve with her but hopefully, not enough to affect her behavior in the long term. When I turn the pages to the positive side of things, I am very certain I have made some lasting impressions on her. I have made it a point of duty to facilitate open and honest discussions with her about any and everything thereby providing the environment to defuse any concerns, fears or events which prevents them from leaving their negative stain.

I have worked with a number of clients who were paralyzed in their adult lives as a result of things they experienced as children/teenagers. They unintentionally turn these incidences into their defining moments and have immense struggles navigating their present day relations. The effects of guilt and it's very close companion shame, can be responsible for seriously hampering the full and authentic expressions of many among us today. No accomplishment, no matter how great seems to diminish the powerful grip guilt and shame can have on an individual. The self-loathing which is a by-product of guilt and shame can cause some to become mean spirited or violent while others turn to self-sabotaging behaviors. The truth is, we needn't suffer in silence if we make the decision to lay down our burdens. Janique summoned the courage (which is the first step) to speak honestly about the situation. She took this step in spite of the consequences she feared (me punishing her or how she perceived I would think of her). Her admission created the space for her to get the help necessary to properly process her actions and access the freedom on the other side of the guilt.

Regarding the song I mentioned earlier I have come to understand the "study war" aspect as follows:

All of us on this journey of life at some point might have done something, said something, or didn't say something that cause us hurt or hurt another person/ animal. Our action or inaction can sow the seed of a life of guilt and shame. We rage war against ourselves when we continue to bear the weight of the guilt or shame we feel around the situation. I implore you to lay down your burdens down by the riverside by apologizing to the person you cause pain (this includes yourself) or talking/writing about the situation. This will help us to forgive ourselves which ultimately ends the self-loathing war we fight within ourselves allowing us to embrace the freedom on the other side.

Worksheet No. 10

1. Have you forgiven yourself for any action on inaction on your part that caused you or another pain? Write about the situation in detail.

2. How has the shame/guilt around this situation affected you in your relationship with yourself and others? Write about this in detail.

3. Highlight what you have done to release yourself of the shame and guilt.

Chapter 19

Puppy Love

My daughter was 10 years old when she told me about her first crush. He was a boy in her class, and according to her, she was "in loooveee" with him. I found her admission quiet fascinating and was eager to hear more about this boy. My first question was, "What do you like about him?"

She smiled and said, "Everything". She went on to say that she liked how he treated her and that he was attentive and handled her with more care and affection in comparison to the other boys in her class. She felt she could have real conversations with him about things that mattered, and he was just "kool" to hang out with. She was grinning from ear to ear when she said, "Mommy he is soooo cute; he has the cutest smile."

I laughed when I noticed how animated she became as she continued to talk about what happened earlier when they had a chance to speak at lunch time. As I watched her and her antics I was reminded of my friends and the joy they expressed when they had a strong liking for someone. Call it infatuation, a crush or love it was very clear to me in that moment that the feeling of liking someone can make you giddy in spite of your age.

The next day I asked her to show me the young man as I followed her to class. She brought me over to him and introduced us, he was very polite and said hi with a bright smile. I instantly saw what Janique found so attractive; outside of his infectious smile, he was well spoken and cute. As the weeks progressed I continued to hear more about this young man, everyday there was a new report about the things he said and did in class and outside of class. He could do no wrong, well that was until a new student was placed in their class.

The new student was smart and friendly and in a very short time she became the object of affection for most of the boys in the class including the boy my daughter was so fond of. All hell broke loose when he started spending more time trying to get to know the new student. Janique was in a tail spin as she couldn't understand the hold the new student seemingly had on the object of her affection. She came home complaining how she didn't understand the connection between them she said she knew for certain that the new student didn't like the young man as much as she (Janique) did. I remember one day she came home and in a fit of absolute frustration she said she wished the girl would just vanish and never return. I felt the moment was the perfect for a heart to heart conversation, so I asked her to tell me what she was really feeling towards the new student. She sat quietly for about three minutes and then started to explain. She told me how she thought the new student was really bright as she aced all her tests and was at the top of the class. She went on to talk about the fact the she actually liked the girl as a person and she spoke to her occasionally She further expressed that the she was feeling more hurt and distress as the young man she liked started spending more time with the new student.

She then said, "Mommy I'm jealous of her. Not only is she smart, but her body is more developed than mine, and he really likes her."

I took a long breath before I responded and I told her that I understood why she felt hurt and related my own story of crushing on a guy who barely noticed me as a teenager. I went on to tell her that everything she felt at the time was natural, but it wasn't necessary to spend time wishing the new student would vanish. I told her that the young man was free to like anyone he wanted to, and she ought to respect that.

She looked up at me and said, "Mom my brain hears what you saying, but my heart is still hurting."

I thought about what she said over the next few days and even told a male acquaintance about it. His first response when I told him she had a crush was if I had reprimanded her. I looked at him quizzically and asked, "What the hell for?"

He emphatically pointed out that at her age it was inappropriate for her to be feeling those things let alone tell me about it. I shook my head in silence as he continued to talk about his own upbringing and how children now-a-days were way too forward and out of line. I quickly got over my surprise at his response and pointed out one of the flaws I observed in terms of how many Jamaican parents raised their children. To date, many struggle to talk to their children about attraction and sex. As a result, children come into this knowledge by questionable sources. What these parents fail to recognized is that our children are little human beings, which is the reason why they are wired to feel attraction and sexual desire even when they don't fully comprehend the whole gamut of what is happening with their minds and bodies. As parents our job is to inform and guide them, so we need to let them feel comfortable talking to us about these things.

I revisited the conversation with Janique about a week after our talk. I casually asked her what was happening with the young man, as she hadn't said another word about him since the last time she mentioned him. She sighed, then she said she was still feeling peeved about the situation. I told her that it would take some time to really get beyond it but that it was important for her to value herself in all of this. She asked me what I meant. I explained that it is when we really like someone that we are more prone to act out of character. I also told her that it was easier to keep the persons we don't like or feel indifferent towards at bay, but that the individual we like was an entirely different matter. We naturally want to spend time with them and tend to find most of the things they do amusing, cool and cute. We want to please them and are a little more open to considering or doing what they asked of us. I explained further that this desire to please had a tendency to reach new heights if we feel desperate to get their attention. Because of this we naturally avail ourselves to them even more and sometimes end up doing things that make us feel bad about ourselves after. I reminded her that it was always more important to love herself first and in so doing she'd be better able to make choices that were in her best interest. I went on to tell her that loving herself meant letting go of people who didn't see her awesomeness. I ended by telling her to never chase anything that was running away from her, that she was enough and that those who loved her would see that..

Worksheet No. 11

1. Did your parents talk to you about attraction?

2. Did you feel comfortable approaching them with questions and concerns about feeling attraction towards another person as a child or teenager?

3. Have you spoken to your child/children about attraction? If you haven't, do you feel nervous about this conversation? Why?

Chapter 20

...And A Child Shall Lead Them

I have noticed that some of us adults spend an inordinate amount of time trying to curtail the natural actions/behaviours of our children. Some parents are constantly behind the children- "correcting" and steering them in another direction. Of course, I understand that we must guide and keep them out of trouble as good parents – that is our role. However, some of us, in our effort to protect, end up stifling the essence out of our little bundle of joy. We often don't notice what we are doing as we attempt to shape and mould them into functional members of society.

One of the things I admired about a friend of mine that has two children was how she allowed them to be themselves and discover their environment without much interference. She'd watched them from a safe distance, offering minimal instructions; this unconventional method allowed the children to thrive and blossom.. Her eldest is 14 and the youngest is 8 now; they are brave, independent, forthright and responsible. I truly believe that her parenting style had everything to do with who they are currently.

I share a similar parenting style to my friend, and I have found that raising my daughter this way has led me to believe that our children are one of our best guides to a joyful and fulfilling life, and here's why:

- Children are the purest manifestation of the term "we are one": They don't recognize social class, culture or ethnicity; they just see another person. Left alone, they engage anyone within close proximity in conversation and play and assess them on the bases of their interaction. It's the adults in their lives that muddle the situation and teach them the idea of separateness. We infuse them with our prejudices some of which are completely unfounded and turn them against each other.

- Children usually make friends easily: I remember taking Janique to a park one day, we were there for about 5 minutes before she noticed a little boy standing a few feet from her. She asked me if it was ok to go over and play with him; I told her yes. Janique ran up to the unsuspecting boy, invaded his person space, said hi and told him she wanted to play with him. He smiled, held her hand, and they both started to run. I stood smiling as they had a good time until we had to go. So many adults struggle to talk to each other and would rather sit in stony silence than initiate light conversation. Some are inept in this department while others choose to remain standoffish (at times this is the case because parents/ guardians counsel them as children not to "mix and mingle").

- Children live in the moment: they are usually completely invested in whatever is going on currently without much thought about what will happen next; for this reason, they enjoy themselves thoroughly. As adults, we allow so much to pass us by the way as we struggle to stay present while being preoccupied with adulting (bills, work, relationship, the past and the future).

- Children are two seconds away from a full out play session: OMG! I've had to run away from my daughter who would pounce on me when I least expected it. She would jump on me when she thought I was looking depressed and instantly brightened my day with a comment like "Let's play and chase the sadness away". She was always right; a good romp usually had me in a fit of laughter and changed my mood immediately. Her readiness to play was a great reminder not to take myself too seriously.

- Children are fearless: as soon as most children start crawling/walking they are busy exploring their environment. They walk towards things and sometimes people with wide-eyed curiosity and wonderment. Some will trod with a little more caution if they had an unpleasant experience with something or someone but tend to continue to embrace new experiences with the same level of enthusiasm. They learn to be fearful because of the things we tell them and by modelling our behavior.

- Children forgive readily: as parents, we have made promises to our children that have gone unfulfilled. We have also said or done things they consider to be hurtful and the kids forgave us readily.

- Children anticipate the things and experiences they want: Promise a child something, and they will hold on to your word with great excitement until it comes to fruition. They believe, with all their being, that they will experience this thing in short order. They imagine it; talk about it, and receive it.

As a society, most of us are attempting to raise our consciousness. We are reading motivational books and are listening to spiritual gurus in an effort to learn how to live more fully – all the while ignoring the example our offsprings provide. Children are head and shoulders above us as conduits of positive energy, and they truly enjoy life. It comes to them naturally to live out loud and most would do just that if we the adults didn't do such an amazing job poisoning them with our fears, broken dreams, unresolved issues and prejudices. My daughter has taught me so much but only because I recognized from early that she was an untainted source of life-giving serum. We can all learn from our children if we practice the "law of allowing", and join them when they go splashing around in a puddle or break out dancing to the music in their head. I also suggest that we join them when they go running naked across the lawn and moon the nosy neighbors. This type of occasional reckless abandon will make you happier – I promise.

Worksheet No. 12

1. How has indulging in the antics of your children helped to make you happier? Explain.

2. Can you see any benefits to being more childlike? (list these benefits and say how it would enhance you).

3. Start doing the things you identified and journal about how it has been impacting how you feel.

Chapter 21

The Birds And The Bees

In 2017, popular Jamaican dancehall artiste, Shawna, released a very controversial song called Equal Rights. The song created quite a buzz as it was glorifying oral sex in Jamaica where there is still public outcry against this form of sexual act. The backlash came from the dancehall fraternity owning to the fact that some of the male dancehall artistes and selectors felt that the song was inappropriate for the genre. Dance hall selectors went as far as boycotting the song, while some artiste decided that they wouldn't perform on shows with Ishawna. Given the pushback she faced because of the song, she became the subject of many newspaper articles and televised discourse.

One Friday I happened to be watching an entertainment show called ER (Entertainment Report) where Ishawna was being interviewed; she spoke about the motivation behind her song "Equal Rights". She stated that in spite of the negative and sometimes violent rhetoric she was dealing with in the dancehall space, many of her detractors were guilty of partaking in cunnilingus. She went on to say oral sex was perfectly naturally and that most women, herself included, enjoyed it. Now, I've always championed the cause for oral sex. In fact, I talk about it on my radio show and even host workshops where I teach people how to do it properly. With that said, I was in agreement with Ishawna and said as much within ear shot of my daughter (unbeknownst to me) who sat a few feet away from the TV listening to something on her phone.

Time Fi Talk Di Tings Dem

Janique took out her ear plugs and asked me if I knew what the song was about. I told her yes. She then asked if I knew the words of the song; I said yes. She had a confused look on her face when she asked the next question. She sat up in the sofa then asked "Mommy are you saying that oral sex is ok?"

I turned to face her and told her that I agreed that it was ok. Her face contorted in absolute disgust. Then and only then did I realize we were about to have *the* sex talk, and it wasn't going to be as planned or thought out, but it would be honest. She had a barrage of questions, such as "how can you say its ok mommy; oral sex is just nasty".

I then asked her why she thought so. She said, "You know the man is putting his mouth on the woman's vagina right? That's nasty". Again, I asked her to explain. At this point, her body was angled away from me which is usually the case when she felt hurt or wronged by my actions. Her response gave me reason to pause.

She said, "So much stuff is constantly coming out of the vagina plus it has a smell". I started by explaining what I told her were the wonders of the vagina. I told her that the vagina was scientifically proven to be cleaner than the mouth primarily because of its ability to self-clean. I went on to explain that "the stuff coming out of it" was referred to as discharge and that was the vagina's way of getting rid of it waste in just the same way the digestive system helps us to process food and get rid of what we no longer needed. I then explain that the scent the vagina carries was also normal unless it was very dirty or there was an infection.

More questions came, but our conversation took a swift and unexpected turn with this question, "Mommy have you had this done to you?"

Under normal circumstances and in another forum (even on radio/TV), my response would have been a resounding, "Hell yes", but my usual exuberance was nowhere to be found. As a matter of fact, for a split second, I considered lying to my daughter. The tension was palpable in the room, and Janique finally turned around to look me in the eye, as I sat dumbfounded for a full minute. Finally, I found my breath and my voice along with it and my response was "Yes". I watched her recoil as my answer seemed to knock the air out of her chest. I registered the scorn, shock and disappointment in her face before she looked away again.

She then said, "You used to be all the way up here for me (lifting her hand to heavens); now, I don't even know how to feel. I never thought that you would do this kind of thing mommy".

My heart was pounding, as things had gotten very intense very fast and nothing in me could have anticipated her reaction. I had been ready for this sex talk since she was about five years old; instead of how I had imagined it would be, I felt like a boxer being pummeled against the rings. This was crazy. It was time to get things in order, so I cleared my throat and asked her to look at me. At first she didn't budge. I said it again, and she looked over her shoulder at me. I asked her to turn completely around. Once we were face to face and looking each other in the eyes, I resumed speaking.   I asked her how well she knew me. When she just sat there looking at me, I asked her how would she describe my cleaning habits? She mumbled that I was constantly cleaning. I asked her if she thought my attention to cleanliness was limited to tidying the house. Before she could answer I told her that oral sex was like a kiss; therefore kissing a clean, healthy vagina was perfectly fine. I told her that oral sex was a form of sexual expression that people shared to pleasure their partner. I explained that some persons don't indulge in oral sex because of the stigma attached to the act in our country but that a lot of persons enjoyed it, even some of the very persons (dancehall artiste included) who spoke out against it.

I could see her starting to loosen up. Evidently, the explanation proved sufficient to her, so she asked me about fellatio. We discussed that then went into the conversation about sex. At this point, I was feeling more relaxed. We spoke about the things that prompted people to have sex (peer pressure, liking someone, curiosity, etc), as well as the attending emotions. Although we had a rocky start, I got the chance to talk to her about sex and not just from the place of penis meeting vagina but the emotions preceding the action and those following. I was very happy to have had the chance to explain more about the vagina and reminded her that I was the best source of this information and that she could always come to me with her questions and concerns.

My parents never had "the talk" with me so I felt it was necessary that my daughter heard it from me. I've noticed how just by virtue of our silence or even the threats that are made, parents have forced some children into early sexual encounters which can cause teenage pregnancy or contracting a sexually transmitted infection. The cycle of silence has been a vicious one and is still pervasive today. During my work as a life coach and wellness practitioner (implementing behaviour modification programs or giving wellness talks) in high schools and universities, it was very clear that many parents never had "the talk" with their children. This fact is further reinforced in my relationship and sensuality coaching practice with women and couples. I discovered in the schools when I had my huddles with the groups I was assigned that their parents/guardians spent more time threatening them about not having sex than they did giving them real information. Then there were those parents who gave them a book leaving them to their own interpretation; or even worse than that, those parents who never said a word causing the children to grow up believing that the topic of sex was a subject they shouldn't broach. As a result, the task of "the talk" has been inadvertently left up to the schools - most of which do a poor and ineffective job of it in an attempt to be administratively correct.

The questions that beg to be asked are:

- Why are we still so uncomfortable talking about sex?

- Why is this perfectly normal exchange still so taboo?

- How can we hope to truly prepare our children for adulthood and never speak to them about attraction, desire, sex and all the emotions it evokes?

As a nation, we have so much work to do as it pertains to edifying ourselves about sex, sexuality and sensuality. It is only when we can have open dialogue about this essential aspect of our lives that we can hope to serve as an honest guide for ourselves and to our children. In so doing, we can finally break the cycle of shame and guilt around this beautiful gift from God.

Worksheet No. 13

1. Did your parents talk to you about sex? If so, did they give you information about sex or threaten you and made you fearful of ever indulging?

2. Do you feel that getting more information about sex/relationships would have been beneficial to you as a child/ teenager and adult?

3. Have you spoken to your children about sex? If not, Why?

4. If you have spoken to your child/ren about sex what did you tell them?

5. Do you allow your children to call their private parts by its biological name?

6. Are you comfortable with your knowledge of sex to share openly with your child/ren?

Chapter 22

Speak Love

Allowing Janique to interact with her father has always brought on mixed emotions for me. The first time he reached out to me to see her she was 8 years old, and I was completely distressed. While it was never my intention to prevent him from seeing her, I felt I needed to protect her from his cavalier approach to parenting. I worried about her forming a bond with him during the period he felt motivated to engage her, and then him vanishing from her life. I was concerned how this would affect her emotionally, given that she had yearned for a relationship with him.

Years later, he remained distant. His sister has been the only member of his family who made any attempts to keep in touch with us regularly. On occasions she'd invited Janique to spend time with their family for the holidays; and even though I really appreciated her kind gesture, I always worried that Janique might be affected by her father being there. I've felt great amounts of uncertainty regarding him having access to her. In the interest of the bigger picture (forming a bond with the other half of the family), however, I facilitate it.

For the first time in 3 years, Janique was invited to his family get-together, which was held in summer 2018, and the same concerns washed over me. After asking her if she wanted to go, I asked her how she felt about seeing him. She said "Mommy I honestly don't feel anything for him; there is just nothing there". She went on to say she had felt great disappointment after he failed to response to her WhatsApp messages. She said "Mommy how hard could it be to just say hello". I sat quietly as she expressed how she got to the place of completely detaching herself from him emotionally. She said "I'm not even angry anymore, I just don't have anything to say to him; I want him to keep his distance." She continued by saying she used to wonder what she had done to him why he didn't want to be a part of her life. At that point I had to fight back tears and the mounting anger I was feeling. Here we were, yet again, trying to figure out why this man didn't want a relationship with his child. I hoped for and wondered if we would ever get to a place where this type of conversation would not stir the negative emotions it did.

In the early years of our separation, I was angry that he had chosen not to be involved her life. As more time passed and the financial burden was solely on me, I was even more angry and frustrated. At times, the frustration changed to all out panic when I wasn't certain how I was going to make ends meet. Even though I would cuss him out mentally, I never made any disparaging comments about him to Janique. I had a business associate who resented her son, because his father had never accepted him as his child. Whenever she was overwhelmed, her son would get an ear full about how worthless his father was and that he was the worst thing that had ever happened to her. She would tell her son that he looked like his wicked father and that he would never amount to anything in life. He moved out of her house the day he turned 18 and haven't spoken to her since.

My business associate story was laced with regret and pain. She said it took her 2 years to get pass the anger she felt when her son moved out and kept his distance from her. After that point, all she felt was guilt as she knew how badly she had hurt him. She was inconsolable, and I couldn't help but cry with her. I know how hard it is to raise a child alone, without any help from the other parent. I, too, have experienced similar moments of anger towards the father of my child, so I could relate to her on some levels. I also understood that she cried because she knew she had wronged her son with her critical comments about his father and felt she had lost him forever as a result. This practice, by mothers and even members of the family, has scarred so many children. Unfortunately, many Jamaican parents are guilty of repeating the popular, but very damaging adage, "you look like you wutliss puppa", to their children. In addition to this, they also hurl cruel comments at them in relation to the missing father or beat them or verbally chastise them or all of the aforementioned. Others have even gone as far as telling the child they were a "mistake".

What many parents have failed to grasp is that the things we say to our children when we are feeling overwhelmed, frustrated and hurt, have lasting effects. The message the child internalizes is that a half of him is bad, no-good and worthless. They can't help but take these comments personal. Therefore, if they are constantly being bombarded with negativity about their father, after a while, it eats away at their confidence. Things can get equally as painful when mothers refuse to talk about the absent father to the children as it becomes difficult for them to form a connection with him. In this scenario (refusing to talk about him or acknowledging his presence), the child struggles to get an idea about themselves and their mannerisms when no information is provided about the other person who was instrumental in their conception.

I thought my ex-husband was a big ass hole for not taking care of his daughter but at no point in our conversations about him did I ever communicate my personal feelings about him to my daughter. All things considered, I chose him. I made the decision to marry him; we made a child, and I refused to make her feel bad about my lousy decision. As far as I was concerned, that is my cross to bear, my lessons to learn - not hers. I felt she was intuitive and observant enough to form her own opinion of him whenever she spent time with him, so I didn't need to colour her perception of him. There was nothing I could do to make him play a role in her life, but I was sure to leave the door open for him to try. I encouraged her to ask any questions she had about him and told her some of the things he did that was funny and good. I told her what I found attractive about him and that some of her behaviours came directly from him. I made sure to do this, because it was important to me that she knew there was more to him than being an absentee dad.

Worksheet No. 14

1. How have you positioned the father of your child/children in their minds? Explain.

2. Do you share the positive aspects of your relationship with your child/dren's father with your child/children? If not, why?

Chapter 23

It Takes Two To Tango

I remember waiting in line at Western Union and someone said something to a lady who was ahead of me. She became visibly upset and started talking loudly about the challenges she was facing getting financial support from the father of her children. I stood silently as she went into a rant about how he had gone missing for years and when she found him, he claimed to be broke. She went on about how hard it was to make ends meet for her three children and that he was the scorn of the earth. I stood silently feeling her pain when another woman chimed in saying the father of her child vanished once she told him she was pregnant, so she has been a single mother for her 13 yr old. She explained how she had to straighten out her son about focusing on his school work to make sure he did not turn into his worthless father.

As I stood there in line listening, the conversation stirred up all kinds of emotions in me. Again, I was reminded that many women were single mothers going above and beyond to take care of their children. So many of the stories sounded the same; the fathers were missing in action and doing little or nothing to assist with raising the children. I had seen it so many times - too many times, in fact. I felt angry and wondered why the government wasn't doing more to make it mandatory for the fathers to financially support their children. I used to ask my lawyer this very same question when I was actively trying to get my ex-husband to make child payment. Why wasn't it possible to just take the child support out of their salary like statutory deduction once they had been brought in front of the court? It seemed so simple to me and thought it would be in the country's best interest to do this as so many of society's ills (crime, violence, maladaptive behaviour in youths) could be directly linked to the fatherless home where mothers struggled to financially care for their children. Single mothers could do so much more by way of being there for their children if the fathers were contributing financially, if nothing else. Personally, it wouldn't be so frustrating trying to supply all my daughter's physical needs, and I know this would be the case for so many other single mothers.

I believe more needs to be done from a policy level to ensure that delinquent fathers are held accountable. I say this knowing full well that we, as women, have a responsibility in this matter to make better choices where men are concerned. Many of us are way too casual when it comes to issues of birth control and practicing safe sex. Then there are those women who believe that the best way to keep a man is to have a child for him. Some go as far as to use the pregnancy as leverage to force the man to marry them. I saw an episode of Iyana Vanzant's show, "Fix my life", where she was doing some work with a man who had sired over 20 children with multiple women. She brought him and all the members of the audience to tears getting him to understand how painful it was for the woman and children he had left to fend for themselves. While I think she did a brilliant job getting him to identify their pain, I felt she should have used the opportunity to speak to many of the single mothers in the audience to become more vigilant in selecting a man to father their child. I know women who meet a man such as the one Iyana was working with knowing the he has 5 or more children that he barely sees or supports and still make the conscious decision to get pregnant for him thinking they would be the one to change him.

Society has spent a lot of time and energy scolding the delinquent fathers as a result some women absolve themselves of any responsibility in the encounter. If we are to rid ourselves of this issue of single parenting, both men and women have to be more selective, diligent and cautious with their sexual behavior. More woman need to be proactive with their sexual encounters and take the necessary measures to protect themselves from unwanted pregnancies. Secondly, women must realize that having a child for a man isn't a guarantee that he will stay in the relationship or get married to them. Lastly it is very important that we take time to get to know our love interests and observe his tendencies towards children (his own or others) Just by observing we can get a picture as to how they view this role of fatherhood and in so doing save our self so much distress.

Worksheet No. 15

Some might find this worksheet uncomfortable however it is a necessary part of taking responsibility for our role in co-creating our situation.

1. Do you believe you have any personal responsibility in being a single mother? Here are some questions to prompt this activity.

2. Did you discuss becoming pregnant with your partner?

3. Did you think the father of your child would be a suitable candidate?

4. Are you usually vigilant about safe sex?

5. If your pregnancy wasn't unplanned what were your reasons for getting pregnant for the father?

Chapter 24

Sharp Left To Cougarville

I came to a realization in my thirties that younger men were very attracted me. I'd be approached in the supermarket, on the beach or at work all the time. My friends found it amusing and kept telling me to act on it, but I'd declined everyone and kept it moving. The thought of entertaining a younger man scared me; hence, I avoided them like the plague. I was convinced that they were even more immature, lost and whoring than their older counterparts. I'd had my fair share of challenges dealing with an older man, so I couldn't fathom being with one younger than me.

A good friend of mine dated and eventually married a younger man and what ensued in their relationship further solidified the belief I had about them. It was the classic case of boy meets girl. Boy was completely enamored and intrigued by the beautiful and progressive girl. The chase began, and he wooed her with his cooking skills and sexual prowess. Girl, over a period of time, falls for boy and in a whirlwind affair the engagement was announced. They got married and within a few months they we expecting. Baby came, and he began to drift; he was now in a hot and heavy relationship with his cell phone which even had a special place in bed with them under his pillow. More and more, there was business that required him to be away from home especially on the weekends and this continued for months until she confronted him. He made an effort for a few days to come home and engage her and their child, but he was back to being missing in action after a short period of pretending to "try".   Over time, the situation worsened until she took the decision to move on. Now I know that this scenario could easily be the case with an older man; but for me, this was further proof, along with the other stories I had heard about younger men, that they were completely off limits for me.

A New Thing

In my best Sophia voice (from the sitcom Golden Girls). *Picture this, Jamaica 2017, I'm conducting a training exercise for a business associate and met a very attractive and forthright young man.   After our training session, a conversation ensued with the trainees about matters of the heart. I sat quietly listening to a young lady talking about the roller coaster relationships she had experienced and the coping mechanisms she felt forced to employ in order to retain some semblance of sanity. Mr. B (the young man) chimed in after a while sharing his relationship challenges, then prompted me to talk about my own. I gave them a synopsis; once I was done talking, then the questions came:*

"How do you feel about a serious relationship as a divorcee?"
"How are you coping with being a single mother?"
"Are you open to marriage again?

After answering the questions as they came, they solicited my feedback on some of their personal concerns regarding relationships. We continued to have spirited conversation for about two hours. During this discourse, I was pleasantly surprised by Mr. B's level of maturity. In the middle of answering one of his questions, he blurted out, "You're gonna be my next wife." I scoffed at him and had a good laugh at his comment.

My Ex- lover and I had been in an on and off relationship for 8 years. I remember telling him once that every time we broke up something inside me closed off to the idea of us. Sometimes it was tiny bits and pieces and at others times large chunks of me. When we separated 4 years ago, I was determined to turn a new page because for as many times as he ended our relationship, I took him back. During one of our separations, I had found one other person attractive enough to have a sexual encounter but decided against doing that, so I only shared myself with my ex-lover because of my comfort level with him. This time around, I was ready and eager for a change. I had finally closed the emotional chapter in our book and tucked said book on a shelf.

Amongst one of the golden nuggets of life that my beloved grandmother had shared with me, was the very ominous comment "Be careful what you ask for, as you just might get it". I'd been asking for a new experience that I spent time thinking about and visualizing. I was happy, really happy with myself and was anticipating a healthy, loving, supportive and satisfying romantic and love-filled relationship as well as an awesome father-figure for my child. It was raining men, and I went out on dates with some; none of them enticed me to have a sexual encounter, but I found a few of them entertaining enough to spend time with.   About two days after the training I received a call from Mr. B. He told me how much he enjoyed our talk after the training and that he would like to take me out. Like I did when he first announced his intention, I scoffed at the idea of going out with him but told him we could chat every now and then. We continued to talk periodically on the phone until I allowed him to pick me up for an early morning TV interview. He took me out after that for breakfast, and we spoke for hours under an umbrella in the pouring rain at one of my favourite cafés. The more time I spent talking to him, the more interesting I found him. He had a very old soul and a consciousness about life that was forged partly through a tumultuous past. He was soulful, attentive, artistic, confident, charming and witty.

Spending time with him was fun and carefree. We did simple things I enjoyed in life, such as trips to the river or cooking up a storm. He took many pictures of me, and for my birthday he sketched me while I lazed about listening to music. After a while, I included my daughter on our trips; they would chat about music for hours on end and became very fond of each other.

The more I got to know him, the more I became very conflicted. Mr. B had made his intentions clear; he wanted us to explore the possibility of having a serious relationship. I, on the other hand, was battling the deeply entrenched perceptions I had about younger men against the unmistakable interest he had sparked in me. Our situation became even more confusing as he was everything I had never found physically appealing before. Whilst he was taller than me, he was very slender (I love me a man with muscles) and hairy (I had never dated a hairy man in life), so much so that he referred to himself as a tropical wolf. Physically he wasn't my type however after a while, none of that mattered to me. Everything about him and this encounter was unfamiliar. He was nonchalant at points about things I felt needed more attention and uptight at other times about things I felt where negligible. In spite of all that, my attraction towards him grew, and I became petrified. I started to wonder what manner of craziness possessed me, as I questioned and dissected the attraction I felt. Was I having a mid-life crisis at 43? But I couldn't deny the way I was feeling (playful, girly and giddy at times in his presence). I was officially frightened and afraid, so I starting pulling back. He noticed right away and sought an explanation and the only way I could describe what was happening was to say that I was having a schizophrenic episode: one side of me (militant Caleen) was screaming, "What the fuck are you doing entertaining this fucking juvenile? Don't you know men his age only want to fuck an older woman for bragging rights? Like seriously get a fucking grip already and send him packing." On the contrary, the other side of me was saying, "Slow down Caleen. There is actually a whole lot of substance here that you haven't encountered with the other men you're dating so slow down; get out of your fucking head, and explore it." I told him that the panic was mounting but I was going to make an effort to go against the grain and stay instead of running.

I sought counsel from my friends who felt this was worth exploring; they encouraged me to live a little and see where it would go. At this point, I was feeling annoyed and miserable. Here I was for the first time in 10 years face to face with a man that actually moved me, but he was well over a decade my junior. Not only that, he was also still trying to figure out his life. Added to that, I felt that he wouldn't be able to give me the things I wanted from a man at this stage of my life. I couldn't explain why I was attracted to him, but I also couldn't put to rest the fears I was wrestling. With that in mind, I told him to go find a younger person who might be better suited, and I took off for higher ground.

The days went by slowly and I missed him terribly, but I kept my distance. My daughter noticed his absence and inquired about it. I told her that as much as I liked him I didn't think he was a best fit for us at this time. She was disappointed and irritated. For the last 3 years she kept asking me when I was going find a man and settle down. She felt that I was too picky and that I kept chasing away good prospects. I started explaining to her that I too was desirous of a relationship but wanted to make sure I made the right decision for both of us. She stopped me mid-sentence and said "I long for a family; I long for a father. I'm tired of us being alone. I watch how hard you work, and I know things would be easier if you had some support. I want that for us Mom, and I see how happy you are with Mr. B so don't let him go because of his age; give him a chance."

After much thought, I contacted Mr. B and asked to see him. I don't know if it was the time apart, but he looked good enough to eat. We chit chatted for a few then got to the meat of the matter. He told me that he felt hurt when I chased him off to find a younger woman and thought that I was acting hastily. I apologized and listened as he opened up about his feelings. He said that he had learnt to not trust his head because it says all kinds of things, some of which are just fear-based. He went on to say that he didn't know where this was going and couldn't make me any promises given the things I needed but he was prepared to do what he could to make this work as everything in him was saying this is where he should be. We sat in silence for a while after that, then I decided to play one of my favourite card game called Spit (Google it). We did that for another hour and ended in a fit of laughter. He reached over and kissed me. In that moment, I made the decision then to let go of my fears and enjoy the experience of being with him. Blessed assurance! It was a delicious experience (smiling from ear to ear at the thought). He was quite an adept lover. He was assertive, attentive, and have the most amazing hands that applied the right amount of pressure in the right places. Merciful fadda don't get me started on his tongue, I could write a thesis on his lips and tongue (helpppppp) a gift from the Gods I swear. Let's just say I was pleasantly surprise as never in my wildest dream did I consider that a younger man could possess this level of control, skill and stamina.

So now I'm officially a cougar. I didn't feel comfortable with the labels of boyfriend/ girlfriend but I honored our interaction and time spent. Whilst I cared deeply for him, there was a large part of me that believed our encounter was meant to be a season, so I cherished it even more.

Our situation taught me a few lessons:-

- In my work with women, I hear so many of them saying they want a new experience/a different kind of man than the one/s they've had before. Some spend too much time fixating on the traits and physical features they want to attract and will only consider a suitor if he fulfils this criteria. I used to tell them to be open and a little less rigid in their outlook. That was great until I had my own experience with a new kind of man. I was immediately out of sorts, IMMEDIATEDLY. I had no prior experience to compare him to physically or otherwise hence my initial response was to tag him as unknown and lock him away in file 13. He was an awesome lesson that showed me the single narrative I had as it pertained to the men I found attractive and how deeply embedded it was. A friend of mine used to say if there was a tall, dark, muscular, bald headed guy in the room, he was going to find me and I him. I spoke about being open and ready for love but unconsciously expected it to look like something I was familiar with. The truth is a NEW experience is just that. IT'S NEW;

HENCE IT WON'T RESEMBLE THE ONES WE'VE HAD BEFORE. This means as women, we should consider dating men outside of our preference looking beyond physical features and get more preoccupied with their energy. It means having conversations not only to ascertain his current stature in life but listening out for his values and morals which speaks to his character.

- Age is just a number: I had to learn this kicking and screaming as yet again I was only mentally prepared to entertain a man no more than 6 years younger than me. I had decided that anything younger was pushing it, and I'd be running the risk of dating an immature child (yes I know that there are men in their 40s and 50s who are ridiculously immature). Mr. B is younger than I am,butttt he's still a man. Yes there were moments when I felt he was being immature. At times, his opinion and behavior could readily be attributed to youthful exuberance and lack of experience. With that being said, he was still a man. This finally registered to me in conversation with one of my friends when I was busy admonishing myself for even entertaining the thought of engaging Mr. B. She made the point that I should be mindful of the terms I used to describe him (like youth) because in spite of the age difference between us, he was still an adult. Her comment created some clarity for me. I didn't need to feel bad or overly confused as I was having a human experience with another human; therefore, what we felt couldn't be contained by our age difference.

- Do you loud and proud: while I lived the term "Do You", I didn't know that I'd be this concerned about people's opinion in this regard. Mr. B was equally as tactile with me in public as behind closed doors, so I never stopped his public display of affection but didn't really reciprocate as I was aware of people's reaction to us. That continued until he called me on it in an argument. He accused me of hardly touching him in public; admittedly, the comment was a hard slap in my face, because it was true. I sat with it for a while then allowed the real me to come out so I started expressing myself more I'd hugged him and kissed him where ever even the neighbours got an eyeful as we behave like love struck teenagers in the parking lot. The more I let go, the more fulfilling our time together became.

Finding someone that I connect with mentally and physically isn't something that happens too often for me`, so the experience with Mr. B has been a wonderful reminder to live my truth, since we only have one life to live.

Worksheet No. 16

1. Do you have a type of man that you typically gravitate towards? If so, what is this type?

2. Have you ever seriously dated a man outside of this typecast?

3. Are you open to a new experience (new type of physical features and disposition) when looking for a relationship?

4. Do you have any preconceived notions about being in a relationship with certain types of men? Explain.

5. Have these notions prevented you from exploring a relationship when approached by that type of man?

Mastery

Chapter 25

Say What You Need To Say

My ex and I separated over 4 years ago. Since that time my daughter has been anxiously waiting for me to start dating someone seriously. She has a keen interest in the men I go with and always want to know what I thought about our date. One day in deep frustration she asked me why I was so picky. I told her that I was choosing for both of us; hence I needed to be careful. I wanted someone who would love and appreciate us, so I was going to take my time until I found a suitable fit. When I was dating Mr. B, she was beside herself when things started to click between us and gave me her blessing to explore it with him.

He had touched our lives in a very special way. After a couple months together, life took him overseas for a few months; it was only then that I realized how much he meant to my daughter and I. We had closed the chapter on our relationship, but I missed him terribly. My daughter spoke about him constantly, which made it harder to release him the way I felt I needed to for closure. While I considered him a friend, we had grown apart during his time away, and it hurt me. When he came back, strangely enough, I couldn't explain it but my feelings couldn't be denied.

I never broached the conversation with him, because I felt he had moved on with his life, and that shit ate away at me. No matter how I tried to dismiss it, something brought it back to the forefront. Janique spoke about him incessantly; they had developed an amazing bond and she felt that the tension between us would affect her relationship with him. She decided to take matters into her hands, and sat me down for a heart to heart discussion. She wanted to know about the cause of the strain between us, so I explained. She said she understood but felt that I had way too much ego in the situation and thought I should reach out to him as some of his behavior was just who he was. I sat listening to my daughter do a splendid job coaching me. She made some brilliant points as she asked me to loosen up and let bygones be bygones and start afresh with him to preserve our friendship.

The weeks dragged on, and he and I spoke periodically. Still, he kept his distance until one night he stopped by, and we talked about the elephant in the room. He explained what had transpired during his time away and why he was distant and apologized when I told him how his behavior impacted me. We talked a little bit more often after that but he was still aloof and I decided I would just leave him alone.

Letting Go

It isn't often that I meet someone that moves me to my core. Yet here I was wondering how and when Mr. B had managed to get into my system the way he had. I couldn't figure it out, and was experiencing a myriad of emotions about it. One day, I would be angry that I had finally connected with someone but couldn't forge ahead with the relationship because I didn't think he could provide the experience I was longing for. The next I would be angry at myself for letting him get this close to me. Those thoughts would open the flood gates of the perceptions I had about dating younger men, and I'd beat up on myself - sometimes a little bit other times a lot. Then I'd feel miserable, just fucking miserable, that things had unfolded the way they did. Then I felt foolish, like a proper jackass. I would ask myself how in God's green earth I had managed to fall for this young man with all his complications. It scared me and made me feel as though I couldn't trust myself to choose a suitable partner. Having thought that, I would then run back into my head trying to figure out what the hell this fucking experience was trying to teach me. I wanted to know why I had attracted him after all this fucking work I had done on me. I was an emotional wreck.

This feeling was like nothing I had ever experienced, and then the dam broke. I felt like my soul was weeping, as I tried frantically to understand the connection I felt to him. It made no sense, but nothing could stop the flow. For three whole days I cried and it sapped all my energy. In a panic, I called a friend hoping that she would somehow help to figure out what the hell was happening to me. She said I needed to call him and tell him how I was feeling, but I couldn't do that. I wasn't sure what to say nor was I sure it would have made any sense. What would I have hoped to achieve? She kept saying that I needed to stop resisting and just trust and surrender, but something in me wouldn't let me. I let the emotions consume me until it dissipated. After a while he started to visit more regularly and eventually the awkwardness started to wane; our conversations became lighter, but I maintained my distance. Janique was polite when he came back, but she was a little indifferent.

Letting go had taken its toll on Janique as well, because she felt really close to him. She thoroughly enjoyed his company as she thought he was real and relatable. She followed him on Instagram, and she would bring some of his posts to my attention. She asked him to come over one evening and when he didn't she came to me to next day saying she didn't understand why things had changed so much between us. I told her that his life was different now and that he had other priorities. I also explained that as much as it hurt, there was nothing we could do the change the situation. I told her to not take it personal and reminded her that everything has a season and that's why we should enjoy the people we love when we have access to them. Something would kick me in chest whenever she mentioned him, and sometimes I would have to fight back the anger or disappointment it stirred up, but I was grateful that she was old enough to understand most of what I was telling her about the situation.

It made me think just how complicated things can get for the children of single mothers, when they form a connection with a man their mom is dating and things don't work out with them. The women aren't the only ones who are emotionally invested, so it can become a real challenge trying to manage the emotions attached when things don't work out. Some children form a deep and meaningful relationship with the man, even considering him in a father-like way, which makes it extremely hard to understand his absence. This is further exacerbated if the child is young, making it harder to understand the dynamics of what's taking place with the adults. The fact that Janique was a teenager didn't minimize the discomfort of not seeing Mr. B. she still talked about him and wanted to involve him in some of our recreational time. This presented a struggle for me on occasion, especially because I was busy trying to work through my feelings and keeping my distance. One day when she had asked if she could call him I had to wrestle back the "Hell no, just leave him alone", but then it dawned on me that I had given her access to him. I had involved her in our outings and play time; therefore, her relationship with him was a by-product our relationship. I had to ask myself if I had the right to stop her from trying to keep in touch. I knew he wasn't a threat to her so there was no real reason to prevent her from contacting him.

Like I did from all the other experiences that came before, I gained some amazing lessons from this situation:

- It's perfectly fine to be vigilant when choosing to expose your children to the persons you are dating.

Depending on the level to which they are exposed to these people, they can form emotional attachment to them that don't break off as soon as you have made the decision to end the relationship. As annoyed as my daughter has been with the length of time it has taken for me to bring a love interest home, I continue to take time in my decision in this regard as a lot is at stake.

- Say what you need to say - tell people how much they matter to you whilst you have them in your life. I'm always preaching to my clients and friends to speak their truth; hence, I was really proud of myself when I was able to articulate to Mr. B how I felt even when my head said "This is crazy; this is futile, don't say a word". Contrary to popular belief it will never hurt to let people know how much they move you. Whether or not this encounter turns into a life time engagement you become more emotionally intelligent and open when you share your feelings.

- Go Live - you have one life to live; therefore, live it today. In spite of our well made plans, our lives unfold one day at a time. We can spend all of our given years trying to make sure we make the right decision and in the process forget to live NOW. Immerse yourself in the people or situations that bring you pleasure as none of us know how long we will continue to have access to them. I've spent a lot of time militantly watching over my heart. Notwithstanding, life has taught me that while it necessary to take care, it is also necessary to just let go; embrace the experiences life has presented you with and LIVE NOW.

- Feel your feelings - your feelings are the outward manifestation of your thoughts conscious or unconscious. Your feelings are the gateway to purging some self-defeating patterns and they help you to have a more intimate relationship with yourself and others. While I think it's important to tell people how they make you feel without any attachment to their response, I also believe it is very important to grieve the loss of a relationship. Cry if you need to. Simply shut away and take time to process the happenings of your interactions. Laugh at the funny stuff; get angry, shout and scream, if that is what's broiling in your belly as this is an important aspect of letting go.

- Honour your child's grieving process - Like I said earlier, once you have exposed your children to the person you're seeing, the possibility exists that they will form a real emotional connection to them. As such, they feel the loss at a very deep level especially if they had identified the person as father figure. It is, therefore, incumbent on you to offer an explanation that doesn't paint the person into a monster if things don't work out. In the event that you and the individual had lived together and have separated, explain this to your child once he/she is of the age to recognize their presence and absence. Be gentle with them when they ask to speak or see the person and facilitate them meeting up periodically, if the person isn't harmful to them.

Worksheet No. 17

1. Do you introduce your child/ren to everyone you date?

2. Is there a criterion that the people you date should attain in order to spend time with your child/ren? If so what is it?

3. Have you ever offered an explanation to your child/ren if the person you introduced them to as a love interest didn't work out?

4. Do you facilitate questions/conversations with your child/ren to gain clarity on the status of the relationship with the love interest you introduce them to?

5. What measures have you put in place to manage the emotional distress of your child/ren when dealing with the loss of the person you were dating?

Chapter 26

We Don't Own Them

We continue to complain that too many men have failed to take up their responsibility as fathers. From all indications, it seems to be a worldwide epidemic, but I must address how mothers have agitated this situation. I must warn you that this view point isn't something we explore when we talk about the parenting dynamics, but it is a very important variable. There is a tendency for some women to become extremely vindictive and spiteful when dealing with the father of the child if they discover that he was cheating or he has ended the relationship to pursue a relationship with another woman. When this happens, they usually take the decision to have SOLE CUSTODY of the child without any legal intervention and make the determination that the man should not see his child OR THEY STIPULATE THE CONDITIONS UNDER WHICH HE CAN SPEND TIME WITH HIS CHILD. This situation is worsened if the man is co-habituating with his new girlfriend or wife. Under these circumstances, it can become next to impossible for the father to have any relationship with his child/ren due to the often time unfolded belief that this new woman is now a threat to the safety of the child.

Some women take it a step further and migrate with the child/ren without the consent of the father in a bid to spite the father for his actions. I can't have this conversation without mentioning the things these women tell the child/ren to justify their actions. They tell them how the father broke up the family by choosing to have a relationship with the new woman, and some will paint the woman out to be a perfect monster who STOLE the father away from them. Of course, to put the icing on the cake, there must be the addition of how this was one big plot on the woman's part to BREAK UP THEIR HAPPY RELATIONSHIP. Suddenly, the father and the woman he is seeing are the villains. These conversations are had with the children over and over; it is had with friends and family within the earshot of the child. The question I keep asking myself is this why would a mother want to hurt her child/ren in this way? Especially if the father has a great relationship with his child/ren. I've often wondered if they realize that in the bid to spite the father, they're also hurting the child/ren?

This situation can get worse as there are the mothers who go as far as preventing the child/ren from speaking to the fathers on the basis of their decision to end the relationship and move on with someone else. These mothers make the child/ren feel guilty for wanting to spend time with their father on the basis of what he did to her the mother and how his actions left the family in shambles. The sad part in this is that sometimes the mothers have the support of her family and friends as she continues to poison the children's minds against their father as a means of pay back for ending the relationship.

Many of us need to understand that WE DON'T OWN PEOPLE. They, therefore, have the God given right to move on if they feel that this relationship is no longer meeting their needs. In an ideal world when people start to feel some level of dissatisfaction in their relationship or a strong attraction towards someone else, they share this with their current partner in a bid to address the concerns. Unfortunately, this isn't always the case in the real world. Most times people chose not to say anything to their partner and drift slowly and silently into the arms of another person. I understand how devastating this can be for the unsuspecting (or suspecting) woman, but this is one of those things that can happen in the love relationship. The truth of the matter is the only thing we can do is to let the man go with grace.

Everyone wants to be afforded this liberty to walk away if they've had a change of heart, and there should be no consequences for doing so. When a man, acting from a place of spite, chooses to physically or emotionally harm a woman as she attempts to end the relationship, he is chastised and ridiculed for being evil and weak. Equal amount of public outcry should be made against mothers who are causing the fathers of their child/ren emotional harm by employing these underhanded tactics to spite the man for walking away from the relationship. Their actions can cause irreparable damage to the relationship the man has with his child/ren therein breaking up the family and for what really?

As a people, we have so much to learn about REAL LOVE and it's manifestation in all of our relationships. It is much easier to practice the law of allowing. Enjoy people when they come into our lives and love them with open arms; clinging and trying to bound people to us has nothing to do with LOVE. More of us need to learn how to arrest our egos. These types of vindictive, petty and negative responses are all by product of the insecurities we have about ourselves. We also need to realize that our destiny is never tied to the person that left, and people leave because they can. Our job is to let them. As single mothers, our job is to play our role to ensure that we can co-parent with the father of our child/ren, once he does not bring them harm in any way. Our job is to ensure that he has a clear path to his child in spite of our differences. Our job is to model behaviours that help to uplift and enhance the lives of our offspring. In doing so, one by one we can make our home, our community our nation and our world a better place.

Chapter 27

Motherhood Isn't Martyrdom

I understand that mothering requires sacrifice, commitment, nurturing and a loving nature, but important in all this giving is the need to strike a balance. I've had clients and friends who've had major struggles in this regard as they experience all kinds of anxiety and guilt when they have to leave their child/ren to take some time for themselves. They beat up on themselves if they're not able to supply all the things they think their child/ren should have and are just generally too hard on themselves, in my opinion.

I'm not certain where some of us got the idea that we must be all things for our children in order to be a good parent; this mind set isn't sustainable. I've been saying "some moms" but feel that at points on the parenting journey, most mothers have found themselves in the position of over-extending. I remember my personal struggle with letting Janique stay with a babysitter. Looking back now, that all-encompassing fear was incapacitating as it meant that I would have Janique all the time to ensure that she was safe. When I was forced to leave her for work, I felt very anxious and literally had to learn to let go one finger at a time.

Someone once told me that I would have to let other caregivers in her life for her own development and for my sanity. That piece of advice was a saving grace. As single mothers there are some things we should prioritize because they are very essential for our self-care. I totally understand that the following can be difficult for some mothers, given their circumstances; however, we should make a concerted effort to factor them into our lives:

Alone time - even an hour or two to do just be with you: sit and think or to enjoy a glass of wine over a book. Catch up on some sleep or your favorite sitcom. Whatever, it is, just do you - whatever that translates to.

Pamper yourself - this is an extension of your alone time and crucial to getting yourself back into the groove. Go get your nails and hair done; go shopping and treat yourself to something that has nothing to do with your child/ren.

Make some adult time - schedule time to spend with your friends without your child/ren. Check out a movie or party. Spend time with your lover and get you some loving.

Exercise - make the time to establish a workout regimen. This can entail walks or run with your child/ren or sessions at the gym. Exercise goes a long way as not only does it help in getting the body in shape, it also triggers the release of the "feel good" neurons, endorphins which can help to stave off depression and keep you in a fairly balanced mood.

Re-engage or start doing things that give you a sense of fulfillment - start a course online, learn a new skill you've been interested in or pick up gardening and carve out the time to get it done.

Practice family planning - I know you might be wondering how this fits in, but I feel this is one of those things we need to pay even closer attention to. Reduce the incidences of a surprise or unwanted pregnancy with the use of appropriate contraceptives.

Form a community - create connections and form friendships that can offer you support in one way or another. Seek these people out for social stimulation, guidance and help as it takes a village to raise a child.

Worksheet No. 18

1. Do you have a routine that replenishes you outside of your child/ren? If not, which one of the above do you feel you need more of?

2. How can you afford yourselves more you time? Really think about this and take the necessary steps to make it a reality.

Chapter 28

They Came Bearing Gifts

In this book, I talked about the three men who impacted my life and that of my child powerfully to date (aside from those who served as great father figures).. I spoke about my ex-husband at length, since his actions floored me on so many levels, but it would be remise of me to just leave the conversation there. I pointed out earlier that my ex-husband provided me some valuable lessons as his actions became the resistance I needed to grow from strength to strength. There is no way I would have discovered the levels of my resourcefulness had it not been for his emotional, physical and financial absence. It would have been difficult for me to see and work through some of the limiting thoughts I had about men had it not been for our encounter. The situation with him forced me to look at me in a way that only this could have and for that gift, I thank him. I'm eternally grateful for the gift from his loins that gave me my beautiful daughter, and I know only he could have given me this amazing child. Lastly, I'm grateful that he provided me with the inspiration to pen this book that helped me to connect so many dots in my life that hopefully will help other women as well.

My first love was a gift like no other. This man opened my eyes to the Eden that existed by giving me access to information that changed my mind-set. He enhanced my life in such an immense way by throwing open the doors to a way of thinking and being that I'll never be the same again. Our relationship took me to dizzying heights and devastating lows that taught me how to value me by choosing situations that are more advantageous to me. I thank him for reflecting back my love so massively. I'm forever blessed by our encounter as our friendship continues to enhance and uplift me.

Mr. B gave me the chance to come out of my head and break my self-imposed barriers and restrictions. In so many ways, he helped me to get beyond my borders. He helped me to break a vicious cycle that got me to the place where I could unequivocally choose me. As I allowed myself to let him go, I saw so clearly that I was releasing more than the connection we shared. My soul/spirit was breaking and releasing an unconscious contract I had signed at some point in my existence that kept me in helper/saviour mode in my love relationships. All this became clear to me, as I cried and bitched and beat myself over attracting this man; but he was what I needed to go deep enough to purge this blockage. I thank him for looking at me, for holding my gaze, sketching me, for the many pictures he took of me, and for entertaining my daughter and I. I thank him, because he gave of his gifts in the way he could. The God in me reverences the God in you.

They all brought me gifts in the good times and in the times that didn't feel so good. They gave me a chance to choose me massively, and for that I'm grateful for having had the encounter.

Worksheet No. 19

I have touched on this issue of reframing the events of the major love relationships in your life in a bid to help us women realize and plug a major energetic leak.

1. Do you feel anger, resentment and disappointment in yourselves over the love interest/s you've attracted? Explain.

2. Write about how the father of your child and any other love interest helped you to evolve.

3. Bless them for having helped you recognize your power and release them with love.

Joy

I was searching, seeking that which eluded me
Looking hard for my completeness
I didn't find it
But
I stumbled upon something different
Sweet and unexpected
Wonderfully small... yet larger than life itself
I found joy[3]

---

[3] *Excerpt for Poem Joy by Chfev*

About The Author

Caleen is a Jamaican Transformational Coach, Motivational Speaker and radio personality. Her formal field of study is Psychology and she is a certified Life and Relationship coach. She has worked extensively in the field of rehabilitation/ behavior modification and personal development.

As a Transformational Coach and Motivational Speaker she facilitates Personal Development and Life Enhancing seminars for organizations within Corporate Jamaica and Government ministries. She helps organizations develop and implement employee wellness programs and operates a private practice under the name Connect Coaching Services where she offers life, relationship and business coaching for individuals and organizations

Caleen is the host of the popular radio show "Life and Love Unleashed" on RJR94 FM and is the founder and C.E.O of **FERVIDA** which is a series of workshops and dance classes she designed to empower women married or unattached on their journey to manifesting a more authentic expression of themselves in all spheres of their lives.

She is the mother of an awesome daughter and a go getter. When she isn't working she loves to travel and explore nature.

She can be reached at cfdiedrick@gmail.com

.